SCHOOLHOUSE DECISIONS OF THE UNITED STATES SUPREME COURT

MAUREEN HARRISON & STEVE GILBERT
EDITORS

EXCELLENT BOOKS
SAN DIEGO, CALIFORNIA

EXCELLENT BOOKS
Post Office Box 927105
San Diego, CA 92192-7105

Publisher's Cataloging-in-Publication Data

Schoolhouse Decisions of the United States Supreme Court/
Maureen Harrison, Steve Gilbert, editors.

p. cm.
Bibliography: p.
Includes Index.
1. United States Supreme Court. 2. Schools - United States - Laws and
Legislation.
I. Title. II. Harrison, Maureen. III. Gilbert, Steve.

KF8742.H24 1997   LC 97-60079
347.'73'26-dc20
[347.30726]
ISBN 0-9628014-9-6

Introduction

There are over 42,000,000 students attending America's elementary and secondary schools. There are almost 2,500,000 teachers working in America's classrooms. The question on the blackboard is: *What happens to the constitutional rights of students and teachers when they walk through the schoolhouse door?*

Schoolhouse Decisions of the United States Supreme Court contains the actual text of thirteen landmark court decisions originating in America's schools, edited into plain non-legal English.

Many of these *Schoolhouse Decisions* have not only directly affected the daily rituals and routines of America's schools; they have become part of the curriculum itself:

The daily flag salute and patriotic pledge, affected by the United States Supreme Court's 1943 landmark *"I Pledge Allegiance"* Decision.

The racial and ethnic composition of every American classroom, affected by the United States Supreme Court's 1954 landmark *School Desegregation* Decision.

The attempt to remove "offensive" books from the school library, affected by the United States Supreme Court's 1982 *Banning School Library Books* Decision.

The continuing controversy over religion's place in public education, affected by the United States Supreme Court's 1962 *School Prayer,* 1963 *Bible Reading,* and 1992 *Graduation Prayer* Decisions.

These and many other equally vital topics of interest to students, teachers, and parents are explored and explained in *Schoolhouse Decisions of the United States Supreme Court.*

Each Supreme Court opinion presented in *Schoolhouse Decisions* is carefully edited into a plain-English version of the original legal text. Judge Learned Hand once wrote: *The language of the law must not be foreign to the ears of those who are to obey it.* The editors have made every effort to make the language of these decisions less "foreign." We have replaced esoteric legalese with plain English. Edited out are long alpha-numeric legal citations and wordy wrangles over abstract points of procedure. Edited in are definitions (standing = the right of a party to participate in a litigation), translations (certiorari = the decision of the Court to review a case), identifications (Appellant = Linda Brown, Appellee = The Board of Education of Topeka, Kansas), and explanations (who the parties were, what laws were at issue, what constitutional issues were involved, where the case originated, how the case reached the court, and what the final decision was). Preceding each edited decision, we provide a history of the case and we note where the unedited decision can be found. The bibliography provides a selected list of further readings on the legal rights and responsibilities of students and teachers. Also included is a complete copy of the United States Constitution, to which every *Schoolhouse Decisions* refers.

The question on the blackboard is: *What happens to the constitutional rights of students and teachers when they walk through the schoolhouse door?* The answers can be found in this text: *Schoolhouse Decisions of the United States Supreme Court.*

M.H. & S.G.

Table Of Contents

Schoolhouse Speech
59

It can hardly be argued that either students or teachers shed their constitutional rights to freedom of speech or expression at the schoolhouse gate.

- Justice Abe Fortas, *Tinker v. Des Moines Schools*

Corporal Punishment
71

Because paddlings are usually inflicted in response to conduct directly observed by teachers in their presence, the risk that a child will be paddled without cause is insignificant.

- Justice Lewis Powell, *Ingraham v. Wright*

Banning School Library Books
93

The right to receive ideas follows ineluctably from the sender's First Amendment right to send them.

- Justice William Brennan, *Island Trees Schools v. Pico*

Searching Students For Drugs
109

A search of a student by a teacher will be justified when there are reasonable grounds for suspecting that the search will turn up evidence that the student has violated either the law or the rules of the school.

- Justice Byron White, *New Jersey v. T.L.O*

"Equal Time" For Creation Science
127

The Louisiana Creationism Act advances a religious doctrine by requiring either the banishment of the theory of evolution from the public school classroom or the presentation of a religious viewpoint that rejects evolution in its entirety.

- Justice William Brennan, *Edwards v. Aguillard*

This book is dedicated in loving memory to
Sadie

*The benefits of education generally diffused through a community are
essential to the preservation of a free government.*
                                                        - Sam Houston

*Enlighten the people generally, and tyranny and oppressions of body
and mind will vanish like evil spirits at the dawn of day.*
                                                        - Thomas Jefferson

"I Pledge Allegiance"
West Virginia Board of Education v. Barnette

I pledge allegiance to the Flag of the United States of America and to the Republic for which it stands; one Nation, indivisible, with liberty and justice for all. **- The Pledge of Allegiance**

On January 9, 1942 the West Virginia Board of Education, in compliance with the State Legislature's mandate to "teach, foster and perpetuate the ideals, principles and spirit of Americanism" ordered a compulsory daily flag salute and pledge. All students were required to participate. Refusal to participate was punishable by expulsion and prosecution for delinquency of the student and a fine and imprisonment for the non-participating student's parent or guardian.

Walter Barnette, a Jehovah's Witness, was one of several parents who, objecting on religious grounds to their children being forced to recite the Pledge of Allegiance, sued the West Virginia Board of Education in Federal Court. The Witnesses, for whom the Bible as the Word of God represented supreme authority, believed that the obligations imposed upon them by the laws of God were superior to those imposed by the laws of men. A similar compulsory flag salute case, the 1940 *Gobitis* case, had already been fought and lost by a Jehovah's Witness in the Supreme Court. Forcing their children to salute the flag, they argued, violated the commandment of Exodus' Chapter 20, Verse 4: *"Thou shalt not make unto thee any graven image . . ."* and Verse 5: *"Thou shall not bow down to [a graven image] . . ."*; they believed the flag to be just such a forbidden "image." The District Court, overturning *Gobitis*, found for Barnette. West Virginia appealed to the United States Supreme Court.

Oral arguments were heard on March 11, 1943 and on June 14, 1943 (Flag Day) the 6-3 decision of the Court was announced by Associate Justice Robert Jackson.

The Barnette Court

Chief Justice Harlan Fiske Stone
Appointed Chief Justice by President Coolidge
Served 1925 - 1946

Associate Justice Owen Roberts
Appointed by President Hoover
Served 1930 - 1945

Associate Justice Hugo Black
Appointed by President Franklin Roosevelt
Served 1937 - 1971

Associate Justice Stanley Reed
Appointed by President Franklin Roosevelt
Served 1938 -1957

Associate Justice Felix Frankfurter
Appointed by President Franklin Roosevelt
Served 1939 - 1962

Associate Justice William O. Douglas
Appointed by President Franklin Roosevelt
Served 1939 - 1975

Associate Justice Frank Murphy
Appointed by President Franklin Roosevelt
Served 1940 - 1949

Associate Justice Robert Jackson
Appointed by President Franklin Roosevelt
Served 1941 - 1954

Associate Justice Wiley Rutledge
Appointed by President Franklin Roosevelt
Served 1943 - 1949

The unedited text of *West Virginia Board of Education v. Barnette* can be found on page 624, volume 319 of *United States Reports*. Our edited text follows.

BOARD OF EDUCATION
v. BARNETTE
June 14, 1943

JUSTICE ROBERT JACKSON: Following the decision by this Court on June 3, 1940, in *Minersville School District v. Gobitis*, the West Virginia legislature amended its statutes to require all schools therein to conduct courses of instruction in history, civics, and in the Constitutions of the United States and of the State "for the purpose of teaching, fostering and perpetuating the ideals, principles and spirit of Americanism, and increasing the knowledge of the organization and machinery of the government." West Virginia's Board of Education was directed, with advice of the State Superintendent of Schools, to "prescribe the courses of study covering these subjects" for public schools. The Act made it the duty of private, parochial and denominational schools to prescribe courses of study "similar to those required for the public schools."

The Board of Education on January 9, 1942, adopted a resolution containing recitals taken largely from the Court's *Gobitis* opinion and ordering that the salute to the flag become "a regular part of the program of activities in the public schools," that all teachers and pupils "shall be required to participate in the salute honoring the Nation represented by the Flag; provided, however, that refusal to salute the Flag be regarded as an Act of insubordination, and shall be dealt with accordingly."

The resolution originally required the "commonly accepted salute to the Flag" which it defined. Objections to the salute as "being too much like Hitler's" were raised by the Parent and Teachers Association, the Boy and Girl Scouts, the Red Cross, and the Federation of Women's Clubs. Some modification appears to have been made in deference to these objections, but no concession was made to Jehovah's Witnesses. What is now required is the "stiff-arm" salute, the saluter to keep the right hand raised with palm turned up while the following is repeated: "I pledge allegiance to the Flag of the United States of America and to the Republic for which it stands; one Nation, indivisible, with liberty and justice for all."

Failure to conform is "insubordination" dealt with by expulsion. Readmission is denied by statute until compliance. Meanwhile the expelled child is "unlawfully absent" and may be proceeded against as a delinquent. His parents or guardians are liable to prosecution, and if convicted are subject to fine not exceeding $50 and jail term not exceeding thirty days.

Appellees, Walter Barnette, Paul Stull, and Lucy McClure, citizens of the United States and of West Virginia, brought suit in the United States District Court for themselves and others similarly situated, asking its injunction [court order to prohibit an act] to restrain enforcement of these laws and regulations against Jehovah's Witnesses. The Witnesses are an unincorporated body teaching that the obligation imposed by law of God is superior to that of laws enacted by temporal government. Their religious beliefs include a literal version of Exodus, Chapter 20, verses 4 and 5, which says: "Thou shalt not make unto thee any graven image, or any likeness of anything that is in heaven above, or that is in the earth beneath, or that is in the water under the earth; thou shalt not bow down thyself to them, nor serve them." They consider that the flag is an "image" within this command. For this reason they refuse to salute it.

Children of this faith have been expelled from school and are threatened with exclusion for no other cause. Officials threaten to send them to reformatories maintained for criminally inclined juveniles. Parents of such children have been prosecuted and are threatened with prosecutions for causing delinquency.

. . . . The cause was submitted . . . to a District Court of three judges. It restrained [halted] enforcement. . . . [T]he Board of Education . . . appeal[ed].

This case calls upon us to reconsider a precedent decision, as the Court throughout its history often has been required to do. Before turning to the *Gobitis* Case, however, it is desirable to notice certain characteristics by which this controversy is distinguished.

The freedom asserted by [Barnette, Stull, and McClure] does not bring them into collision with rights asserted by any other individual. It is such conflicts which most frequently require intervention of the State to determine where the rights of one end and those of another begin. But the refusal of these persons to participate in the ceremony does not interfere with or deny rights of others to do so. Nor is there any question in this case that their behavior is peaceable and orderly. The sole conflict is between authority and rights of the individual. The State asserts power to condition access to public education on making a prescribed sign and profession and at the same time to coerce attendance by punishing both parent and child. The latter stand on a right of self-determination in matters that touch individual opinion and personal attitude.

As the present Chief Justice [Harlan Fiske Stone] said in dissent in the *Gobitis* Case, the State may "require teaching by instruction and study of all in our history and in the structure and organization of our government, including the guaranties of civil liberty, which tend to inspire patriotism and love of country." Here, however, we are dealing with a compulsion of students to declare a belief. They are not merely made acquainted with the flag salute so that they may be informed as to what it is or even what it means. The issue here is whether this slow and easily neglected route to aroused loyalties constitutionally may be short-cut by substituting a compulsory salute and slogan. . . .

There is no doubt that, in connection with the pledges, the flag salute is a form of utterance. Symbolism is a primitive but effective way of communicating ideas. The use of an emblem or flag to symbolize some system, idea, institution, or personality, is a short cut from mind to mind. Causes and nations, political parties, lodges and ecclesiastical groups seek to knit the loyalty of their followings to a flag or banner, a color or design. The State announces rank, function, and authority through crowns and maces, uniforms and black robes; the church speaks through the Cross, the Crucifix, the altar and shrine, and clerical raiment. Symbols of State often convey political ideas just as religious symbols come to convey theological ones. Associated with many of these symbols are appropriate gestures of acceptance or respect: a salute, a bowed or bared head, a bended knee. A person gets from a symbol the meaning he puts into it, and what is one man's comfort and inspiration is another's jest and scorn.

Over a decade ago Chief Justice Hughes led this Court in holding that the display of a red flag as a symbol of opposition by peaceful and legal means to organized government was protected by the free speech guaranties of the Constitution. Here it is the State that employs a flag as a symbol of adherence to government as presently organized. It requires the individual to communicate by word and sign his acceptance of the political ideas it thus bespeaks. Objection to this form of communication when coerced is an old one, well known to the framers of the Bill of Rights.

It is also to be noted that the compulsory flag salute and pledge requires affirmation of a belief and an attitude of mind. It is not clear whether the regulation contemplates that pupils forego any contrary convictions of their own and become unwilling converts to the prescribed ceremony or whether it will be acceptable if they simulate assent by words without belief and by a gesture barren of meaning. It is now a commonplace that censorship or suppression of expression of opinion is tolerated by our Constitution only when the expression presents a clear and present danger of action of a kind the State is empowered to prevent and punish. It would seem that involuntary affirmation could be commanded only on even more immediate and urgent grounds than silence. But here the power of compulsion is invoked without any allegation that remaining passive during a flag salute ritual creates a clear and present danger that would justify an effort even to muffle expression. To sustain [uphold] the compulsory flag salute we are required to say that a Bill of Rights which guards the individual's right to speak his own mind, left it open to public authorities to compel him to utter what is not in his mind.

Whether the First Amendment to the Constitution will permit officials to order observance of ritual of this nature does not depend upon whether as a voluntary exercise we would think it to be good, bad or merely innocuous. Any credo of nationalism is likely to include what some disapprove or to omit what others think essential, and to give off different overtones as it takes on different accents or interpretations. If official power exists to coerce acceptance of any patriotic creed, what it shall contain cannot be decided by courts, but must be largely discretionary with the ordaining authority, whose power to prescribe would no doubt include power to amend. Hence validity of the asserted power to force an American citizen publicly to profess any statement of belief or to engage in any ceremony of assent to one, presents questions of power that must be considered independently of any idea we may have as to the utility of the ceremony in question.

Nor does the issue as we see it turn on one's possession of particular religious views or the sincerity with which they are held. While religion supplies [Barnette, Stull, and McClure's] motive for enduring the discomforts of making the issue in this case, many citizens who do not share these religious views hold such a compulsory rite to infringe constitutional liberty of the individual. It is not necessary to inquire whether nonconformist beliefs will exempt from the duty to salute unless we first find power to make the salute a legal duty.

The *Gobitis* decision, however, *assumed*, as did the argument in that case and in this, that power exists in the State to impose the flag salute discipline upon school children in general. The Court only examined and rejected a claim based on religious beliefs of immunity from an unquestioned general rule. The question which underlies the flag salute controversy is whether such a ceremony so touching matters of opinion and political attitude may be imposed upon the individual by official authority under powers committed to any political organization under our Constitution. We examine rather than assume existence of this power and . . . re-examine specific grounds assigned for the *Gobitis* decision.

1. It was said that the flag-salute controversy confronted the Court with "the problem which Lincoln cast in memorable dilemma: 'Must a government of necessity be too *strong* for the liberties of its people, or too *weak* to maintain

its own existence?'" and that the answer must be in favor of strength.

We think these issues may be examined free of pressure or restraint growing out of such considerations.

It may be doubted whether Mr. Lincoln would have thought that the strength of government to maintain itself would be impressively vindicated by our confirming power of the state to expel a handful of children from school. Such oversimplification, so handy in political debate, often lacks the precision necessary to postulates of judicial reasoning. If validly applied to this problem, the utterance cited would resolve every issue of power in favor of those in authority and would require us to override every liberty thought to weaken or delay execution of their policies.

Government of limited power need not be anemic government. Assurance that rights are secure tends to diminish fear and jealousy of strong government, and by making us feel safe to live under it makes for its better support. Without promise of a limiting Bill of Rights it is doubtful if our Constitution could have mustered enough strength to enable its ratification. To enforce those rights today is not to choose weak government over strong government. It is only to adhere as a means of strength to individual freedom of mind in preference to officially disciplined uniformity for which history indicates a disappointing and disastrous end.

The subject now before us exemplifies this principle. Free public education, if faithful to the ideal of secular instruction and political neutrality, will not be partisan or enemy of any class, creed, party, or faction. If it is to impose any ideological discipline, however, each party or denomination must seek to control, or failing that, to weaken the influence of the educational system. Observance of the limitations of the Constitution will not weaken government in the field appropriate for its exercise.

2. It was also considered in the *Gobitis* Case that functions of educational officers in states, counties and school districts were such that to interfere with their authority "would in effect make us the school board for the country."

The Fourteenth Amendment, as now applied to the States, protects the citizen against the State itself and all of its creatures - Boards of Education not excepted. These have, of course, important, delicate, and highly discretionary functions, but none that they may not perform within the limits of the Bill of Rights. That they are educating the young for citizenship is reason for scrupulous protection of Constitutional freedoms of the individual, if we are not to strangle the free mind at its source and teach youth to discount important principles of our government as mere platitudes.

Such Boards are numerous and their territorial jurisdiction often small. But small and local authority may feel less sense of responsibility to the Constitution, and agencies of publicity may be less vigilant in calling it to account. The action of Congress in making flag observance voluntary and respecting the conscience of the objector in a matter so vital as raising the Army contrasts sharply with these local regulations in matters relatively trivial to the welfare of the nation. There are village tyrants as well as village Hampdens, but none who acts under color of law is beyond reach of the Constitution.

3. The *Gobitis* opinion reasoned that this is a field "where courts possess no marked and certainly no controlling competence," that it is committed to the legislatures as well as the courts to guard cherished liberties and that it is con-

stitutionally appropriate to "fight out the wise use of legislative authority in the forum of public opinion and before legislative assemblies rather than to transfer such a contest to the judicial arena," since all the "effective means of inducing political changes are left free."

The very purpose of a Bill of Rights was to withdraw certain subjects from the vicissitudes of political controversy, to place them beyond the reach of majorities and officials and to establish them as legal principles to be applied by the courts. One's right to life, liberty, and property, to free speech, a free press, freedom of worship and assembly, and other fundamental rights may not be submitted to vote; they depend on the outcome of no elections.

In weighing arguments of the parties it is important to distinguish between the due process clause of the Fourteenth Amendment as an instrument for transmitting the principles of the First Amendment and those cases in which it is applied for its own sake. The test of legislation which collides with the Fourteenth Amendment, because it also collides with the principles of the First, is much more definite than the test when only the Fourteenth is involved. Much of the vagueness of the due process clause disappears when the specific prohibitions of the First become its standard. The right of a State to regulate, for example, a public utility may well include, so far as the due process test is concerned, power to impose all of the restrictions which a legislature may have a "rational basis" for adopting. But freedoms of speech and of press, of assembly, and of worship may not be infringed on such slender grounds. They are susceptible of restriction only to prevent grave and immediate danger to interests which the state may lawfully protect. It is important to note that while it is the Fourteenth Amendment which bears directly upon the State it is the more specific limiting principles of the First Amendment that finally governs this case.

Nor does our duty to apply the Bill of Rights to assertions of official authority depend upon our possession of marked competence in the field where the invasion of rights occurs. True, the task of translating the majestic generalities of the Bill of Rights, conceived as part of the pattern of liberal government in the eighteenth century, into concrete restraints on officials dealing with the problems of the twentieth century, is one to disturb self-confidence. These principles grew in soil which also produced a philosophy that the individual was the center of society, that his liberty was attainable through mere absence of governmental restraints, and that government should be entrusted with few controls and only the mildest supervision over men's affairs. We must transplant these rights to a soil in which the laissez-faire concept or principle of non-interference has withered at least as to economic affairs, and social advancements are increasingly sought through closer integration of society and through expanded and strengthened governmental controls. These changed conditions often deprive precedents of reliability and cast us more than we would choose upon our own judgment. But we act in these matters not by authority of our competence but by force of our commissions. We cannot, because of modest estimates of our competence in such specialties as public education, withhold the judgment that history authenticates as the function of this Court when liberty is infringed.

4. Lastly, and this is the very heart of the *Gobitis* opinion, it reasons that "national unity is the basis of national security," that the authorities have "the right to select appropriate means for its attainment," and hence reaches the conclusion that such compulsory measures toward "national

unity" are constitutional. Upon the verity of this assumption depends our answer in this case.

National unity as an end which officials may foster by persuasion and example is not in question. The problem is whether under our Constitution compulsion as here employed is a permissible means for its achievement.

Struggles to coerce uniformity of sentiment in support of some end thought essential to their time and country have been waged by many good as well as by evil men. Nationalism is a relatively recent phenomenon but at other times and places the ends have been racial or territorial security, support of a dynasty or regime, and particular plans for saving souls. As first and moderate methods to attain unity have failed, those bent on its accomplishment must resort to an ever increasing severity. As governmental pressure toward unity becomes greater, so strife becomes more bitter as to whose unity it shall be. Probably no deeper division of our people could proceed from any provocation than from finding it necessary to choose what doctrine and whose program public educational officials shall compel youth to unite in embracing. Ultimate futility of such attempts to compel coherence is the lesson of every such effort from the Roman drive to stamp out Christianity as a disturber of its pagan unity, the Inquisition, as a means to religious and dynastic unity, the Siberian exiles as a means to Russian unity, down to the fast failing efforts of our present totalitarian enemies. Those who begin coercive elimination of dissent soon find themselves exterminating dissenters. Compulsory unification of opinion achieves only the unanimity of the graveyard.

It seems trite but necessary to say that the First Amendment to our Constitution was designed to avoid these ends by avoiding these beginnings. There is no mysticism in the

American concept of the State or of the nature or origin of its authority. We set up government by consent of the governed, and the Bill of Rights denies those in power any legal opportunity to coerce that consent. Authority here is to be controlled by public opinion, not public opinion by authority.

The case is made difficult not because the principles of its decision are obscure but because the flag involved is our own. Nevertheless, we apply the limitations of the Constitution with no fear that freedom to be intellectually and spiritually diverse or even contrary will disintegrate the social organization. To believe that patriotism will not flourish if patriotic ceremonies are voluntary and spontaneous instead of a compulsory routine is to make an unflattering estimate of the appeal of our institutions to free minds. We can have intellectual individualism and the rich cultural diversities that we owe to exceptional minds only at the price of occasional eccentricity and abnormal attitudes. When they are so harmless to others or to the State as those we deal with here, the price is not too great. But freedom to differ is not limited to things that do not matter much. That would be a mere shadow of freedom. The test of its substance is the right to differ as to things that touch the heart of the existing order.

If there is any fixed star in our constitutional constellation, it is that no official, high or petty, can prescribe what shall be orthodox in politics, nationalism, religion, or other matters of opinion or force citizens to confess by word or act their faith therein. If there are any circumstances which permit an exception, they do not now occur to us.

We think the action of the local authorities in compelling the flag salute and pledge transcends constitutional limitations on their power and invades the sphere of intellect and spirit which it is the purpose of the First Amendment to our Constitution to reserve from all official control.

The decision of this Court in *Minersville School District v. Gobitis* and the holdings of those few per curiam [by the whole court, without one author] decisions which preceded and foreshadowed it are overruled, and the judgment enjoining [halting] enforcement of the West Virginia Regulation is affirmed [upheld].

School Desegregation
Brown v. Board of Education of Topeka, Kansas

In the early 1950's the public education systems of twenty-one states and the District of Columbia were either required or permitted to practice racial segregation in public education. The NAACP's Legal Defense Fund, headed by Thurgood Marshall, sought to end legal segregation in education by challenging the U.S. Supreme Court to reverse its 1896 *Plessy* "separate but equal" segregation decision.

In 1952 eight-year-old Linda Brown was forced to attend an all-black Topeka, Kansas public school 21 blocks from her home when there was an all-white public school only 5 blocks away. Her father, Oliver Brown, sued Topeka's Board of Education in Federal Court to force them to admit Linda to the local all-white school. The NAACP's Legal Defense Fund, which represented Linda, based their argument for the reversal of the *Plessy* "separate but equal" segregation doctrine on the Fourteenth Amendment's Equal Protection Clause, which says: *No state shall make or enforce any law which shall deny any person within its jurisdiction the equal protection of the laws.* Final oral arguments were heard on December 7-9, 1953 and on May 17, 1954 Chief Justice Earl Warren announced the Court's 9-0 *Brown I* decision.

The *Brown v. Board of Education* school desegregation decision threw the segregation in education policies of twenty-one states and the District of Columbia into chaos. The Supreme Court, to begin the process of school desegregation in these jurisdictions, allowed the states directly impacted to argue before the Court how fast the *Brown* decision would be implemented. Oral arguments were held before the Court on April 11-14, 1955 and on May 31, 1955 Chief Justice Earl Warren announced the Court's 9-0 *Brown II* decision.

The Brown Court

Chief Justice Earl Warren
Appointed by President Eisenhower
Served 1953 - 1969

Associate Justice Hugo Black
Appointed by President Franklin Roosevelt
Served 1937 - 1971

Associate Justice Stanley Reed
Appointed by President Franklin Roosevelt
Served 1938 - 1957

Associate Justice Felix Frankfurter
Appointed by President Franklin Roosevelt
Served 1939 - 1962

Associate Justice William O. Douglas
Appointed by President Franklin Roosevelt
Served 1939 - 1975

Associate Justice Robert Jackson
Appointed by President Franklin Roosevelt
Served 1941 - 1954

Associate Justice Harold Burton
Appointed by President Truman
Served 1945 - 1958

Associate Justice Tom Clark
Appointed by President Truman
Served 1949 - 1967

Associate Justice Sherman Minton
Appointed by President Truman
Served 1949 - 1956

The unedited text of *Brown v. Board of Education I* and *Brown v. Board of Education II* can be found on page 483, volume 347 and page 294, volume 349 of *United States Reports*. Our edited text follows.

BROWN v. BOARD OF EDUCATION I
May 17, 1954

CHIEF JUSTICE EARL WARREN: These cases come to us from the States of Kansas, South Carolina, Virginia, and Delaware. They are premised on different facts and different local conditions, but a common legal question justifies their consideration together in this consolidated opinion.

In each of the cases, minors of the Negro race [called the plaintiffs], through their legal representatives, seek the aid of the courts in obtaining admission to the public schools of their community on a nonsegregated basis. In each instance, they had been denied admission to schools attended by white children under laws requiring or permitting segregation according to race. This segregation was alleged to deprive the plaintiffs of the equal protection of the laws under the Fourteenth Amendment. In each of the cases other than the Delaware case, a three-judge federal district court denied relief to the plaintiffs on the so-called "separate but equal" doctrine announced by this Court in [the 1896 decision] *Plessy v. Ferguson.* Under that doctrine, equality of treatment is accorded when the races are provided substantially equal facilities, even though these facilities be separate. In the Delaware case, the Supreme Court of Delaware adhered to that doctrine, but ordered that the plaintiffs be admitted to the white schools because of their superiority to the Negro schools.

The plaintiffs contend that segregated public schools are not "equal" and cannot be made "equal," and that hence they are deprived of the equal protection of the laws. Because of the obvious importance of the question presented, the Court [agreed to hear the case]. Argument was heard in the 1952 Term, and reargument was heard this Term on certain questions [asked] by the Court.

Reargument was largely devoted to the circumstances surrounding the adoption of the Fourteenth Amendment in 1868. It covered exhaustively consideration of the Amendment in Congress, ratification by the states, then existing practices in racial segregation, and the views of proponents and opponents of the Amendment. This discussion and our own investigation convince us that, although these sources cast some light, it is not enough to resolve the problem with which we are faced. At best, they are inconclusive. The most avid proponents of the post-[Civil] War Amendments undoubtedly intended them to remove all legal distinctions among "all persons born or naturalized in the United States." Their opponents, just as certainly, were antagonistic to both the letter and the spirit of the Amendments and wished them to have the most limited effect. What others in Congress and the state legislatures had in mind cannot be determined with any degree of certainty.

An additional reason for the inconclusive nature of the Amendment's history, with respect to segregated schools, is the status of public education at that time. In the South, the movement toward free common schools, supported by general taxation, had not yet taken hold. Education of white children was largely in the hands of private groups. Education of Negroes was almost non-existent, and practically all of the race were illiterate. In fact, any education of Negroes was forbidden by law in some states. Today, in contrast, many Negroes have achieved outstanding success in the arts and sciences as well as in the business and professional world. It is true that public school education at the time of the Amendment had advanced further in the North, but the effect of the Amendment on Northern States was generally ignored in the Congressional debates. Even in the

North, the conditions of public education did not approximate those existing today. The curriculum was usually rudimentary; ungraded schools were common in rural areas; the school term was but three months a year in many states; and compulsory school attendance was virtually unknown. As a consequence, it is not surprising that there should be so little in the history of the Fourteenth Amendment relating to its intended effect on public education.

In the first cases in this Court construing [interpreting] the Fourteenth Amendment, decided shortly after its adoption, the Court interpreted it as [prohibiting] all state-imposed discriminations against the Negro race. The doctrine of "separate but equal" did not make its appearance in this Court until 1896 in the case of *Plessy v. Ferguson*, involving not education but transportation. American courts have since labored with the doctrine for over half a century. In this Court, there have been six cases involving the "separate but equal" doctrine in the field of public education. In *Cumming v. County Board of Education*, and *Gong Lum v. Rice*, the validity of the doctrine itself was not challenged. In more recent cases, all on the graduate school level, inequality was found in that specific benefits enjoyed by white students were denied to Negro students of the same educational qualifications. In none of these cases was it necessary to re-examine the doctrine to grant relief to the Negro plaintiff. And in *Sweatt v. Painter*, the Court expressly reserved decision on the question whether *Plessy v. Ferguson* should be held inapplicable to public education.

In [these] cases, that question is directly presented. Here, unlike *Sweatt v. Painter*, there are findings [in lower State and Federal Courts] that the Negro and white schools involved have been equalized, or are being equalized, with respect to buildings, curricula, qualifications and salaries of teachers, and other "tangible" factors. Our decision, therefore, cannot turn on merely a comparison of these tangible factors in the Negro and white schools involved in each of the cases. We must look instead to the effect of segregation itself on public education.

In approaching this problem, we cannot turn the clock back to 1868 when the Amendment was adopted, or even to 1896 when *Plessy v. Ferguson* was written.

We must consider public education in the light of its full development and its present place in American life throughout the Nation. Only in this way can it be determined if segregation in public schools deprives these plaintiffs of the equal protection of the laws.

Today, education is perhaps the most important function of state and local governments. Compulsory school attendance laws and the great expenditures for education both demonstrate our recognition of the importance of education to our democratic society. It is required in the performance of our most basic public responsibilities, even service in the armed forces. It is the very foundation of good citizenship. Today it is a principal instrument in awakening the child to cultural values, in preparing him for later professional training, and in helping him to adjust normally to his environment. In these days, it is doubtful that any child may reasonably be expected to succeed in life if he is denied the opportunity of an education. Such an opportunity, where the state has undertaken to provide it, is a right which must be made available to all on equal terms.

We come then to the question presented: Does segregation of children in public schools solely on the basis of race, even though the physical facilities and other "tangible" factors may be equal, deprive the children of the minority group of equal educational opportunities? We believe that it does.

In *Sweatt v. Painter*, in finding that a segregated law school for Negroes could not provide them equal educational opportunities, this Court relied in large part on "those qualities which are incapable of objective measurement but which make for greatness in a law school." In *McLaurin v. Oklahoma State Regents*, the Court, in requiring that a Negro admitted to a white graduate school be treated like all other students, again resorted to intangible considerations: ". . . his ability to study, to engage in discussions and exchange views with other students, and, in general, to learn his profession." Such considerations apply with added force to children in grade and high schools. To separate them from others of similar age and qualifications solely because of their race generates a feeling of inferiority as to their status in the community that may affect their hearts and minds in a way unlikely ever to be undone. The effect of this separation on their educational opportunities was well stated by a finding in the Kansas case by a court which nevertheless felt compelled to rule against the Negro plaintiffs:

> "Segregation of white and colored children in public schools has a detrimental effect upon the colored children. The impact is greater when it has the sanction of the law; for the policy of separating the races is usually interpreted as denoting the inferiority of the negro group. A sense of inferiority affects the motivation of a child to learn. Segregation with the sanction of law, therefore, has a tendency to [retard] the educational and mental development of negro children and to deprive them of some of the benefits they would receive in a racial[ly] integrated school system."

Whatever may have been the extent of psychological knowledge at the time of *Plessy v. Ferguson,* this finding is amply supported by modern authority. Any language in *Plessy v. Ferguson* contrary to this finding is rejected.

We conclude that in the field of public education the doctrine of "separate but equal" has no place. Separate educational facilities are inherently unequal. Therefore, we hold that the plaintiffs and others similarly situated for whom the actions have been brought are, by reason of the segregation complained of, deprived of the equal protection of the laws guaranteed by the Fourteenth Amendment. This disposition makes unnecessary any discussion whether such segregation also violates the Due Process Clause of the Fourteenth Amendment.

Because these are class actions [where one person represents a larger group], because of the wide applicability of this decision, and because of the great variety of local conditions, the formulation of decrees [orders of the court] in these cases presents problems of considerable complexity. On reargument, the consideration of appropriate relief [how to end school segregation] was necessarily subordinated to the primary question - the constitutionality of segregation in public education. We have now announced that such segregation is a denial of the equal protection of the laws. In order that we may have the full assistance of the parties in formulating decrees, the cases will be restored to the docket [put on the Court's calendar], and the parties are requested to present further argument on [these issues] for the reargument this Term. The Attorney General of the United States is again invited to participate. The Attorneys General of the states requiring or permitting segregation in public education will also be permitted to appear as [friends of the Court]. . . . It is so ordered.

BROWN v. BOARD OF EDUCATION II
May 31, 1955

CHIEF JUSTICE EARL WARREN: [This case was] decided on May 17, 1954. The [opinion] of that date, declaring the fundamental principle that racial discrimination in public education is unconstitutional, [is] incorporated herein by reference. All provisions of federal, state, or local law requiring or permitting such discrimination must yield to this principle. There remains for consideration the manner in which relief is to be accorded.

. . . . In view of the nationwide importance of the decision, we invited the Attorney General of the United States and the Attorneys General of all states requiring or permitting racial discrimination in public education to present their views on that question. The parties, the United States, and the States of Florida, North Carolina, Arkansas, Oklahoma, Maryland, and Texas filed briefs and participated in the oral argument.

These presentations were informative and helpful to the Court in its consideration of the complexities arising from the transition to a system of public education freed of racial discrimination. The presentations also demonstrated that substantial steps to eliminate racial discrimination in public schools have already been taken, not only in some of the communities in which these cases arose, but in some of the states appearing as amici curiae [friends of the court], and in other states as well. Substantial progress has been made in the District of Columbia and in the communities in Kansas and Delaware involved in this litigation. The defendants in the cases coming to us from South Carolina and Virginia are awaiting the decision of this Court concerning relief.

Full implementation of these constitutional principles may require solution of varied local school problems. School authorities have the primary responsibility for elucidating, assessing, and solving these problems; courts will have to consider whether the action of school authorities constitutes good faith implementation of the governing constitutional principles. Because of their proximity to local conditions and the possible need for further hearings, the courts which originally heard these cases can best perform this judicial appraisal. Accordingly, we believe it appropriate to remand [return] the cases to those courts.

In fashioning and effectuating the decrees, the courts will be guided by equitable principles. Traditionally, equity [fairness] has been characterized by a practical flexibility in shaping its remedies and by a facility for adjusting and reconciling public and private needs. These cases call for the exercise of these traditional attributes of equity power. At stake is the personal interest of the plaintiffs [Brown and the others] in admission to public schools as soon as practicable on a nondiscriminatory basis. To effectuate this interest may call for elimination of a variety of obstacles in making the transition to school systems operated in accordance with the constitutional principles set forth in our May 17, 1954, decision. Courts of equity may properly take into account the public interest in the elimination of such obstacles in a systematic and effective manner. But it should go without saying that the vitality of these constitutional principles cannot be allowed to yield simply because of disagreement with them.

While giving weight to these public and private considerations, the courts will require that the defendants [the Board of Education] make a prompt and reasonable start toward full compliance with our May 17, 1954, ruling. Once such a start has been made, the courts may find that additional time is necessary to carry out the ruling in an effective manner. The burden rests upon the [School Board] to establish that such time is necessary in the public interest and is consistent with good faith compliance at the earliest practicable date. To that end, the courts may consider problems related to administration, arising from the physical condition of the school plant, the school transportation system, personnel, revision of school districts and attendance areas into compact units to achieve a system of determining admission to the public schools on a nonracial basis, and revision of local laws and regulations which may be necessary in solving the foregoing problems. They will also consider the adequacy of any plans the [School Board] may propose to meet these problems and to effectuate a transition to a racially nondiscriminatory school system. During this period of transition, the courts will retain jurisdiction of these cases.

The [judgment] below . . . [is] accordingly reversed and the [case is] remanded to the District [Court] to take such proceedings and enter such orders and decrees consistent with this opinion as are necessary and proper to admit to public schools on a racially nondiscriminatory basis with all deliberate speed [Brown and the others]. . . . It is so ordered.

School Prayer
Engel v. Vitale

Almighty God, we acknowledge our dependence upon Thee, and we beg Thy blessings upon us, our parents, our teachers, and our Country.
- The New York "Regents' Prayer"

The New York Board of Regents, a governmental agency charged with supervision of New York State's public school system, composed a "non-denominational" official school prayer, which they recommended for daily classroom recitation. Any student not wanting to join in the recitation of the "Regents' Prayer" was permitted to either remain silent or leave the classroom. The Regents said of their official prayer: "We believe that this [prayer] will be subscribed to by all men and women of good will, and we call upon all of them to aid in giving life to our program."

The School Board of New Hyde Park, Long Island, New York, directed, as recommended by the New York State Regents, that its principals require their students to recite the official "Regents' Prayer" aloud at the beginning of each school day. Several New Hyde Park parents, including Stephen Engel, objected to the daily recitation of the "Regents' Prayer" in their children's classroom. Alleging that it was a violation of the First Amendment's Establishment Clause, they brought suit against William Vitale, Jr., President of the School Board. Three New York Courts - the Nassau County Court, the New York Court of Appeals, and the New York Supreme Court - all found for the School District. Engel appealed to the U.S. Supreme Court.

Oral arguments were heard in *Engel v. Vitale* on April 3, 1962 and the 6-1 decision of the Court was announced on June 25, 1962 by Associate Justice Hugo Black.

The Engel Court

Chief Justice Earl Warren
Appointed Chief Justice by President Eisenhower
Served 1953 - 1969

Associate Justice Hugo Black
Appointed by President Franklin Roosevelt
Served 1937 - 1971

Associate Justice William O. Douglas
Appointed by President Franklin Roosevelt
Served 1939 - 1975

Associate Justice Tom Clark
Appointed by President Truman
Served 1949 - 1967

Associate Justice John Marshall Harlan
Appointed by President Eisenhower
Served 1955 -1971

Associate Justice William Brennan
Appointed by President Eisenhower
Served 1956 - 1990

Associate Justice Potter Stewart
Appointed by President Eisenhower
Served 1958 - 1981

The unedited text of *Engel v. Vitale* can be found on page 421, volume 370 of *United States Reports*. Our edited text follows.

ENGEL v. VITALE
June 25, 1962

JUSTICE HUGO BLACK: The respondent Board of Education of Union Free School District No. 9, New Hyde Park, New York, acting in its official capacity under state law, directed the School District's principal to cause the following prayer to be said aloud by each class in the presence of a teacher at the beginning of each school day:

> "Almighty God, we acknowledge our dependence upon Thee, and we beg Thy blessings upon us, our parents, our teachers and our Country."

This daily procedure was adopted on the recommendation of the State Board of Regents, a governmental agency created by the State Constitution to which the New York Legislature has granted broad supervisory, executive, and legislative powers over the State's public school system. These state officials composed the prayer which they recommended and published as a part of their "Statement on Moral and Spiritual Training in the Schools," saying: "We believe that this Statement will be subscribed to by all men and women of good will, and we call upon all of them to aid in giving life to our program."

Shortly after the practice of reciting the Regents' prayer was adopted by the School District, the parents of ten pupils brought this action in a New York State Court insisting that use of this official prayer in the public schools was contrary to the beliefs, religions, or religious practices of both themselves and their children. Among other things, these parents challenged the constitutionality of both the state law authorizing the School District to direct the use of prayer in public schools and the School District's regulation ordering the recitation of this particular prayer on the ground that these actions of official governmental agencies violate that part of the First Amendment of the Federal Constitution which commands that "Congress shall make no law respecting an establishment of religion" - a command which was "made applicable to the State of New York by the Fourteenth Amendment of the said Constitution." The New York Court of Appeals, over the dissents of Judges Dye and Fuld, sustained [let stand] an order of the lower state courts which had upheld the power of New York to use the Regents' prayer as a part of the daily procedures of its public schools so long as the schools did not compel any pupil to join in the prayer over his or his parents' objection. We granted certiorari [agreed to] review this important decision involving rights protected by the First and Fourteenth Amendments.

We think that by using its public school system to encourage recitation of the Regents' prayer, the State of New York has adopted a practice wholly inconsistent with the Establishment Clause. There can, of course, be no doubt that New York's program of daily classroom invocation of God's blessings as prescribed in the Regents' prayer is a religious activity. It is a solemn avowal of divine faith and supplication for the blessings of the Almighty. The nature of such a prayer has always been religious, none of the [members of the School Board] has denied this and the trial court expressly so found:

> "The religious nature of prayer was recognized by Jefferson and has been concurred in by theological writers, the United States Supreme Court and State courts and administrative officials, including New York's Commissioner of Education. A committee of the New York Legislature has agreed.

"The Board of Regents . . . , the [School Board] and [other interested parties] all concede the religious nature of prayer, but seek to distinguish this prayer because it is based on our spiritual heritage. . . ."

The petitioners contend among other things that the state laws requiring or permitting use of the Regents' prayer must be struck down as a violation of the Establishment Clause [of the First Amendment] because that prayer was composed by governmental officials as a part of a governmental program to further religious beliefs. For this reason, petitioners argue, the State's use of the Regents' prayer in its public school system breaches the constitutional wall of separation between Church and State. We agree with that contention since we think that the constitutional prohibition against laws respecting an establishment of religion must at least mean that in this country it is no part of the business of government to compose official prayers for any group of the American people to recite as a part of a religious program carried on by government.

It is a matter of history that this very practice of establishing governmentally composed prayers for religious services was one of the reasons which caused many of our early colonists to leave England and seek religious freedom in America. The Book of Common Prayer, which was created under governmental direction and which was approved by Acts of Parliament in 1548 and 1549, set out in minute detail the accepted form and content of prayer and other religious ceremonies to be used in the established, tax-supported Church of England. The controversies over the Book and what should be its content repeatedly threatened to disrupt the peace of that country as the accepted forms of prayer in the established church changed with the views of the particular ruler that happened to be in control at the time. Powerful groups representing some of the varying religious views of the people struggled among themselves to impress their particular views upon the Government and obtain amendments of the Book more suitable to their respective notions of how religious services should be conducted in order that the official religious establishment would advance their particular religious beliefs. Other groups, lacking the necessary political power to influence the Government on the matter, decided to leave England and its established church and seek freedom in America from England's governmentally ordained and supported religion.

It is an unfortunate fact of history that when some of the very groups which had most strenuously opposed the established Church of England found themselves sufficiently in control of colonial governments in this country to write their own prayers into law, they passed laws making their own religion the official religion of their respective colonies. Indeed, as late as the time of the Revolutionary War, there were established churches in at least eight of the thirteen former colonies and established religions in at least four of the other five. But the successful Revolution against English political domination was shortly followed by intense opposition to the practice of establishing religion by law. This opposition crystallized rapidly into an effective political force in Virginia where the minority religious groups such as Presbyterians, Lutherans, Quakers and Baptists had gained such strength that the adherents to the established Episcopal Church were actually a minority themselves. In 1785-1786, those opposed to the established Church, led by James Madison and Thomas Jefferson, who, though themselves not members of any of these dissenting religious groups, opposed all religious establishments by law on grounds of principle, obtained the enactment of the famous "Virginia Bill for Religious Liberty" by which all religious groups were placed on an equal footing so far as the State was concerned. Similar though less far-reaching legislation was being considered and passed in other States.

By the time of the adoption of the Constitution, our history shows that there was a widespread awareness among many Americans of the dangers of a union of Church and State. These people knew, some of them from bitter personal experience, that one of the greatest dangers to the freedom of the individual to worship in his own way lay in the Government's placing its official stamp of approval upon one particular kind of prayer or one particular form of religious services. They knew the anguish, hardship and bitter strife that could come when zealous religious groups struggled with one another to obtain the Government's stamp of approval from each King, Queen, or Protector that came to temporary power. The Constitution was intended to avert a part of this danger by leaving the government of this country in the hands of the people rather than in the hands of any monarch. But this safeguard was not enough. Our Founders were no more willing to let the content of their prayers and their privilege of praying whenever they pleased be influenced by the ballot box than they were to let these vital matters of personal conscience depend upon the succession of monarchs. The First Amendment was added to the Constitution to stand as a guarantee that neither the power nor the prestige of the Federal Government would be used to control, support or influence the kinds of prayer the American people can say - that the people's religions must not be subjected to the pressures of government for change each time a new political administration is elected to office. Under that Amendment's prohibition against governmental establishment of religion, as reinforced by the provisions of the Fourteenth Amendment, government in this country, be it state or federal, is without power to prescribe by law any particular form of prayer which is to be used as an official prayer in carrying on any program of governmentally sponsored religious activity.

There can be no doubt that New York's state prayer program officially establishes the religious beliefs embodied in the Regents' prayer. The [Board's] argument to the contrary, which is largely based upon the contention that the Regents' prayer is "non-denominational" and the fact that the program, as modified and approved by state courts, does not require all pupils to recite the prayer but permits those who wish to do so to remain silent or be excused from the room, ignores the essential nature of the program's constitutional defects. Neither the fact that the prayer may be denominationally neutral nor the fact that its observance on the part of the students is voluntary can serve to free it from the limitations of the Establishment Clause, as it might from the Free Exercise Clause, of the First Amendment, both of which are operative against the States by virtue of the Fourteenth Amendment. Although these two clauses may in certain instances overlap, they forbid two quite different kinds of governmental encroachment upon religious freedom. The Establishment Clause, unlike the Free Exercise Clause, does not depend upon any showing of direct governmental compulsion and is violated by the enactment of laws which establish an official religion whether those laws operate directly to coerce nonobserving individuals or not. This is not to say, of course, that laws officially prescribing a particular form of religious worship do not involve coercion of such individuals. When the power, prestige and financial support of government is placed behind a particular religious belief, the indirect coercive pressure upon religious minorities to conform to the prevailing officially approved religion is plain. But the purposes underlying the Establishment Clause go much further than that. Its first and most immediate purpose rested on the belief that a union of government and religion tends to destroy government and to degrade religion. The history of governmentally established religion, both in England and in this country, showed that whenever government had allied itself with one particular form of religion, the inevitable result had been that it had incurred the hatred, disrespect and even contempt of those who held contrary beliefs. That same history showed that many people had lost their respect for any religion that had relied upon the support of government to spread its faith. The Establishment Clause thus stands as an expression of principle on the part of the Founders of our Constitution that religion is too personal, too sacred, too holy, to permit its "unhallowed perversion" by a civil magistrate. Another purpose of the Establishment Clause rested upon an awareness of the historical fact that governmentally established religions and religious persecutions go hand in hand. The Founders knew that only a few years after the Book of Common Prayer became the only accepted form of religious services in the established Church of England, an Act of Uniformity was passed to compel all Englishmen to attend those services and to make it a criminal offense to conduct or attend religious gatherings of any other kind - a law which was consistently flouted by dissenting religious groups in England and which contributed to widespread persecutions of people like John Bunyan who persisted in holding "unlawful [religious] meetings . . . to the great disturbance and distraction of the good subjects of this kingdom. . . ." And they knew that similar persecutions had received the sanction of law in several of the colonies in this country soon after the establishment of official religions in those colonies. It was in large part to get completely away from this sort of systematic religious persecution that the Founders brought into being our Nation, our Constitution, and our Bill of Rights with its prohibition against any governmental establishment of religion. The New York laws officially prescribing the Regents' prayer are inconsis-

tent both with the purposes of the Establishment Clause
and with the Establishment Clause itself.

It has been argued that to apply the Constitution in such a
way as to prohibit state laws respecting an establishment of
religious services in public schools is to indicate a hostility
toward religion or toward prayer. Nothing, of course, could
be more wrong. The history of man is inseparable from the
history of religion. And perhaps it is not too much to say
that since the beginning of that history many people have
devoutly believed that "More things are wrought by prayer
than this world dreams of." It was doubtless largely due to
men who believed this that there grew up a sentiment that
caused men to leave the cross-currents of officially established state religions and religious persecution in Europe
and come to this country filled with the hope that they
could find a place in which they could pray when they
pleased to the God of their faith in the language they chose.
And there were men of this same faith in the power of
prayer who led the fight for adoption of our Constitution
and also for our Bill of Rights with the very guarantees of
religious freedom that forbid the sort of governmental activity which New York has attempted here. These men
knew that the First Amendment, which tried to put an end
to governmental control of religion and of prayer, was not
written to destroy either. They knew rather that it was
written to quiet well-justified fears which nearly all of them
felt arising out of an awareness that governments of the
past had shackled men's tongues to make them speak only
the religious thoughts that government wanted them to
speak and to pray only to the God that government wanted
them to pray to. It is neither sacreligious nor antireligious to
say that each separate government in this country should
stay out of the business of writing or sanctioning official
prayers and leave that purely religious function to the peo-

ple themselves and to those the people choose to look to for religious guidance.

It is true that New York's establishment of its Regents' prayer as an officially approved religious doctrine of that State does not amount to a total establishment of one particular religious sect to the exclusion of all others - that, indeed, the governmental endorsement of that prayer seems relatively insignificant when compared to the governmental encroachments upon religion which were commonplace two hundred years ago. To those who may subscribe to the view that because the Regents' official prayer is so brief and general there can be no danger to religious freedom in its governmental establishment, however, it may be appropriate to say in the words of James Madison, the author of the First Amendment:

> "[I]t is proper to take alarm at the first experiment on our liberties. . . . Who does not see that the same authority which can establish Christianity, in exclusion of all other Religions, may establish with the same ease any particular sect of Christians, in exclusion of all other Sects? That the same authority which can force a citizen to contribute three pence only of his property for the support of any one establishment, may force him to conform to any other establishment in all cases whatsoever?"

The judgment of the Court of Appeals of New York is reversed and the cause remanded [sent back to the appropriate lower court for reruling].

Bible Reading In The Public Schools
Abington Schools v. Schempp
Murray v. Curlett

The Commonwealth of Pennsylvania required by law that each school day begin with: "At least ten verses from the Holy Bible read, without comment." Students not wishing to participate in the classroom reading could be excused upon written request of their parents. Edward and Sidney Schempp of Philadelphia, members of the Unitarian Church, had all three of their children enrolled in the Abington Schools. The Schempps sued the Abington Schools in U.S. District Court, contending that the Compulsory Bible Readings Law was in violation of the First Amendment's Religion Clauses. The U.S. District Court struck down Pennsylvania's Bible Reading Law. The Abington Schools appealed to the United States Supreme Court.

The Baltimore School Commission required by rule that each school day begin with: "Reading, without comment, of a chapter of the Holy Bible and/or the use of the Lord's Prayer." Students not wishing to participate in the classroom reading could be excused upon written request of their parents. Baltimore parent Madalyn Murray and her school-age son, William Murray, atheists, sued the Baltimore School Board in State Court, contending that the Baltimore Schools' Compulsory Bible Readings Rule was a violation of the First Amendment's Religion Clauses. The Maryland Court of Appeals upheld Baltimore's Bible Reading Law. The Murrays appealed to the United States Supreme Court.

Oral arguments were heard in *Abington Schools v. Schempp* and *Murray v. Curlett* on February 27-28, 1963 and the 8-1 decision of the Court was announced on June 17, 1963 by Associate Justice Tom Clark.

The Abington/Murray Court

Chief Justice Earl Warren
Appointed Chief Justice by President Eisenhower
Served 1953 - 1969

Associate Justice Hugo Black
Appointed by President Franklin Roosevelt
Served 1937 - 1971

Associate Justice William O. Douglas
Appointed by President Franklin Roosevelt
Served 1939 - 1975

Associate Justice Tom Clark
Appointed by President Truman
Served 1949 - 1967

Associate Justice John Marshall Harlan
Appointed by President Eisenhower
Served 1955 - 1971

Associate Justice William Brennan
Appointed by President Eisenhower
Served 1956 - 1990

Associate Justice Potter Stewart
Appointed by President Eisenhower
Served 1958 - 1981

Associate Justice Byron White
Appointed by President Kennedy
Served 1962 - 1993

Associate Justice Arthur Goldberg
Appointed by President Kennedy
Served 1962 - 1965

The unedited text of *Abington Schools v. Schempp* and *Murray v. Curlett* can be found on page 203, volume 374 of *United States Reports*. Our edited text follows.

ABINGTON SCHOOLS v. SCHEMPP
MURRAY v. CURLETT
June 17, 1963

JUSTICE THOMAS CLARK: Once again we are called upon to consider the scope of the provision of the First Amendment to the United States Constitution which declares that "Congress shall make no law respecting an establishment of religion, or prohibiting the free exercise thereof. . . ." [This case] present[s] the [issue] in the context of state action requiring that schools begin each day with readings from the Bible. . . . In light of the history of the First Amendment and of our [previous decisions] interpreting and applying its requirements, we hold that the practices at issue and the laws requiring them are unconstitutional under the Establishment Clause, as applied to the States through the Fourteenth Amendment.

The Commonwealth of Pennsylvania by law requires that "At least ten verses from the Holy Bible shall be read, without comment, at the opening of each public school on each school day. Any child shall be excused from such Bible reading, or attending such Bible reading, upon the written request of his parent or guardian." The Schempp family, husband and wife and two of their three children, brought suit to enjoin [stop] enforcement of the statute, contending that their rights under the Fourteenth Amendment to the Constitution of the United States are, have been, and will continue to be violated unless this statute be declared unconstitutional as violative of these provisions of the First Amendment. They sought to [stop] the . . . school district, [where] the Schempp children attend school, and its officers and the Superintendent of Public Instruction of the Commonwealth from continuing to conduct such readings and recitation of the Lord's Prayer in the public schools of the district pursuant to the statute. . . .

Edward Lewis Schempp, his wife Sidney, and their children, Roger and Donna, are of the Unitarian faith and are members of the Unitarian Church in Germantown, Philadelphia, Pennsylvania, where they, as well as another son, Ellory, regularly attend religious services. The latter was originally a party but having graduated from the school system . . . was voluntarily dismissed from the action. The other children attend the Abington Senior High School. . . .

On each school day at the Abington Senior High School between 8:15 and 8:30 a.m., while the pupils are attending their home rooms or advisory sections, opening exercises are conducted pursuant to the statute. The exercises are broadcast into each room in the school building through an intercommunications system and are conducted under the supervision of a teacher by students attending the school's radio and television workshop. Selected students from this course gather each morning in the school's workshop studio for the exercises, which include readings by one of the students of 10 verses of the Holy Bible, broadcast to each room in the building. This is followed by the recitation of the Lord's Prayer, likewise over the intercommunications system, but also by the students in the various classrooms, who are asked to stand and join in repeating the prayer in unison. The exercises are closed with the flag salute and such pertinent announcements as are of interest to the students. Participation in the opening exercises, as directed by the statute, is voluntary. The student reading the verses from the Bible may select the passages and read from any version he chooses, although the only copies furnished by the school are the King James version, copies of which were circulated to each teacher by the school district. During the period in which the exercises have been conducted the King James, the Douay and the Revised Standard versions of the Bible have been used, as well as the Jewish Holy Scriptures. There are no prefatory statements, no questions asked or solicited, no comments or explanations made and no interpretations given at or during the exercises. The students and parents are advised that the student may absent himself from the classroom or, should he elect to remain, not participate in the exercises.

It appears from the record that in schools not having an intercommunications system the Bible reading and the recitation of the Lord's Prayer were conducted by the homeroom teacher, who chose the text of the verses and read them herself or had students read them in rotation or by volunteers. This was followed by a standing recitation of the Lord's Prayer, together with the Pledge of Allegiance to the flag by the class in unison and a closing announcement of routine school items of interest.

At the first trial Edward Schempp and the children testified as to specific religious doctrines purveyed by a literal reading of the Bible "which were contrary to the religious beliefs which they held and to their familial teaching." The children testified that all of the doctrines to which they referred were read to them at various times as part of the exercises. Edward Schempp testified at the second trial that he had considered having Roger and Donna excused from attendance at the exercises but decided against it for several reasons, including his belief that the children's relationships with their teachers and classmates would be adversely affected.

. . . . The trial court, in striking down the practices and the statute requiring them, made specific findings of fact that the children's attendance at Abington Senior High School is compulsory and that the practice of reading 10 verses from the Bible is also compelled by law. It also found that:

> "The reading of the verses, even without comment, possesses a devotional and religious character and constitutes in effect a religious observance. The devotional and religious nature of the morning exercises is made all the more apparent by the fact that the Bible reading is followed immediately by a recital in unison by the pupils of the Lord's Prayer. The fact that some pupils, or theoretically all pupils, might be excused from attendance at the exercises does not mitigate the obligatory nature of the ceremony for [the statute] unequivocally requires the exercises to be held every school day in every school in the Commonwealth. The exercises are held in the school buildings and perforce are conducted by and under the authority of the local school authorities and during school sessions. Since the statute requires the reading of the 'Holy Bible,' a Christian document, the practice . . . prefers the Christian religion. The record demonstrates that it was the intention of . . . the Commonwealth . . . to introduce a religious ceremony into the public schools of the Commonwealth."

. . . . It is true that religion has been closely identified with our history and government. As we said in *Engel v. Vitale,* "The history of man is inseparable from the history of religion. And . . . since the beginning of that history many people have devoutly believed that 'More things are wrought by prayer than this world dreams of.'" In *Zorach v. Clauson,* we gave specific recognition to the proposition that "[w]e are a religious people whose institutions presuppose a Supreme Being." The fact that the Founding Fathers believed devotedly that there was a God and that the unalienable rights of man were rooted in Him is clearly evidenced in their writings, from the Mayflower Compact to the Constitution itself. This background is evidenced today in our public life through the continuance in our oaths of office from the Presidency to the Alderman of the final supplication, "So help me God." Likewise each House of the Congress provides through its Chaplain an opening prayer, and the sessions of this Court are declared open by the crier in a short ceremony, the final phrase of which invokes the grace of God. Again, there are such manifestations in our military forces, where those of our citizens who are under the restrictions of military service wish to engage in voluntary worship. Indeed, only last year an official survey of the country indicated that 64% of our people have church membership, while less than 3% profess no religion whatever. It can be truly said, therefore, that today, as in the beginning, our national life reflects a religious people who, in the words of Madison, are "earnestly praying, as . . . in duty bound, that the Supreme Lawgiver of the Universe . . . guide them into every measure which may be worthy of his [blessing. . . .]"

This is not to say, however, that religion has been so identified with our history and government that religious freedom is not likewise as strongly imbedded in our public and private life. Nothing but the most telling of personal experiences in religious persecution suffered by our forebears could have planted our belief in liberty of religious opinion any more deeply in our heritage. It is true that this liberty frequently was not realized by the colonists, but this is readily accountable by their close ties to the Mother Country. However, the views of Madison and Jefferson, preceded by Roger Williams, came to be incorporated not only in the Federal Constitution but likewise in those of most of our States. This freedom to worship was indispensable in a country whose people came from the four quarters of the earth and brought with them a diversity of religious opinion. Today authorities list 83 separate religious bodies, each with membership exceeding 50,000, existing among our people, as well as innumerable smaller groups.

Almost a hundred years ago in *Minor v. Board of Education of Cincinnati*, Judge Alphonso Taft . . . stated the ideal of our people as to religious freedom as one of "absolute equality before the law, of all religious opinions and sects. . . .

"The government is neutral, and, while protecting all, it prefers none. . . ."

Before examining this "neutral" position in which the Establishment and Free Exercise Clauses of the First Amendment place our Government it is well that we discuss the reach of the Amendment under the [case before] this Court.

First, this Court has decisively settled that the First Amendment's mandate that "Congress shall make no law respecting an establishment of religion, or prohibiting the free exercise thereof" has been made wholly applicable to the States by the Fourteenth Amendment. Twenty-three years ago in *Cantwell v. Connecticut*, this Court . . . said:

> "The fundamental concept of liberty embodied in that [Fourteenth] Amendment embraces the liberties guaranteed by the First Amendment. The First Amendment declares that Congress shall make no law respecting an establishment of religion or prohibiting the free exercise thereof. The Fourteenth Amendment has rendered the legislatures of the states as incompetent as Congress to enact such laws. . . ."

In a series of cases since *Cantwell* the Court has repeatedly reaffirmed that doctrine, and we do so now.

Second, this Court has rejected unequivocally the contention that the Establishment Clause forbids only governmental preference of one religion over another. Almost 20 years ago in *Everson*, the Court said that "[n]either a state nor the Federal Government can set up a church. Neither can pass laws which aid one religion, aid all religions, or prefer one religion over another." And Justice Jackson, dissenting, agreed:

> "There is no answer to the proposition . . . that the effect of the religious freedom Amendment to our Constitution was to take every form of propagation of religion out of the realm of things which could directly or indirectly be made public business and thereby be supported in whole or in part at taxpayers' expense. . . . This freedom was first in the Bill of Rights because it was first in the forefathers' minds; it was set forth in absolute terms, and its strength is its rigidity."

Further, [Justices] Rutledge, Frankfurter, Jackson and Burton declared:

> "The [First] Amendment's purpose was not to strike merely at the official establishment of a single sect, creed or religion, outlawing only a formal relation such as had prevailed in England and some of the colonies. Necessarily it was to uproot all such relationships. But the object was broader than separating church and state in this narrow sense. It was to create a complete and permanent separation of the spheres of religious activity and

civil authority by comprehensively forbidding every form of public aid or support for religion."

The same conclusion has been firmly maintained ever since that time, and we reaffirm it now.

. . . . Justice Roberts for the Court in *Cantwell v. Connecticut* . . . said . . . "Freedom of conscience and freedom to adhere to such religious organization or form of worship as the individual may choose cannot be restricted by law. On the other hand, it safeguards the free exercise of the chosen form of religion. Thus the [First] Amendment embraces two concepts - freedom to believe and freedom to act. The first is absolute but, in the nature of things, the second cannot be."

A half dozen years later in *Everson v. Board of Education,* this Court, through Justice Black, stated that the "scope of the First Amendment . . . was designed forever to suppress" the establishment of religion or the prohibition of the free exercise thereof. In short, the Court held that the Amendment "requires the state to be a neutral in its relations with groups of religious believers and non-believers; it does not require the state to be their adversary. State power is no more to be used so as to handicap religions than it is to favor them."

And Justice Jackson, in dissent, declared that public schools are organized "on the premise that secular education can be isolated from all religious teaching so that the school can inculcate all needed temporal knowledge and also maintain a strict and lofty neutrality as to religion. The assumption is that after the individual has been instructed in worldly wisdom he will be better fitted to choose his religion."

Moreover, all of the four dissenters, speaking through Justice Rutledge, agreed that "Our constitutional policy . . . does not deny the value or the necessity for religious training, teaching or observance. Rather it secures their free exercise. But to that end it does deny that the state can undertake or sustain them in any form or degree. For this reason the sphere of religious activity, as distinguished from the secular intellectual liberties, has been given the two fold protection and, as the state cannot forbid, neither can it perform or aid in performing the religious function. The dual prohibition makes that function altogether private."

. . . . [I]n 1961 in *McGowan v. Maryland* . . . Chief Justice Warren . . . said:

> "But, the First Amendment, in its final form, did not simply bar a congressional enactment *establishing a church; it forbade all laws respecting an establishment of religion.* Thus, this Court has given the Amendment a 'broad interpretation . . . in the light of its history and the evils it was designed forever to suppress. . . .'"

And Justice Black . . . in *Torcaso [v. Watkins]* . . . used this language:

> "We repeat and again reaffirm that neither a State nor the Federal Government can constitutionally force a person 'to profess a belief or disbelief in any religion.' Neither can constitutionally pass laws or impose requirements which aid all religions as against non-believers, and neither can aid those religions based on a belief in the existence of God as against those religions founded on different beliefs."

Finally, in *Engel v. Vitale*, only last year, these principles were so universally recognized that the Court without the citation of a single case and over the sole dissent of Justice Stewart, reaffirmed them. The Court found the 22-word prayer used in "New York's program of daily classroom invocation of God's blessings as prescribed in the Regents' prayer . . . [to be] a religious activity." It held that "it is no part of the business of government to compose official prayers for any group of the American people to recite as a part of a religious program carried on by government."

. . . . And in further elaboration the Court found that the "first and most immediate purpose [of the Establishment Clause] rested on the belief that a union of government and religion tends to destroy government and to degrade religion." When government, the Court said, allies itself with one particular form of religion, the inevitable result is that it incurs "the hatred, disrespect and even contempt of those who held contrary beliefs."

The wholesome "neutrality" of which this Court's cases speak thus stems from a recognition of the teachings of history that powerful sects or groups might bring about a fusion of governmental and religious functions or a concert or dependency of one upon the other to the end that official support of the State or Federal Government would be placed behind the tenets of one or of all orthodoxies. This the Establishment Clause prohibits. And a further reason for neutrality is found in the Free Exercise Clause, which recognizes the value of religious training, teaching and observance and, more particularly, the right of every person to freely choose his own course with reference thereto, free of any compulsion from the state. This the Free Exercise Clause guarantees. Thus, as we have seen, the two clauses may overlap. . . . [T]o withstand the strictures of the Establishment Clause there must be a secular legislative purpose and a primary effect that neither advances nor inhibits religion. The Free Exercise Clause . . . withdraws from legislative power, state and federal, the exertion of any restraint on the free exercise of religion. Its purpose is to secure religious liberty in the individual by prohibiting any invasions thereof by civil authority. Hence it is necessary in a free exercise case for one to show the coercive effect of the enactment as it operates against him in the practice of his religion. The distinction between the two clauses is apparent - a violation of the Free Exercise Clause is predicated on coercion while the Establishment Clause violation need not be so attended.

Applying the Establishment Clause principles to [this case] we find that [Pennsylvania is] requiring the selection and reading at the opening of the school day of verses from the Holy Bible and the recitation of the Lord's Prayer by the students in unison. These exercises are prescribed as part of the curricular activities of students who are required by law to attend school. They are held in the school buildings under the supervision and with the participation of teachers employed in those schools. . . . The trial court . . . has found that such an opening exercise is a religious ceremony and was intended by the State to be so. We agree with the trial court's finding as to the religious character of the exercises. Given that finding, the exercises and the law requiring them are in violation of the Establishment Clause.

. . . . The conclusion follows that . . . the [law] require[s] religious exercises and such exercises are being conducted in direct violation of the rights of the [Schempps]. Nor are these required exercises mitigated by the fact that students may absent themselves upon parental request, for that fact furnishes no defense to a claim of unconstitutionality under the Establishment Clause. Further, it is no defense to urge that the religious practices here may be relatively minor encroachments on the First Amendment. The breach of neutrality that is today a trickling stream may all too soon become a raging torrent and, in the words of Madison, "it is proper to take alarm at the first experiment on our liberties."

It is insisted that unless these religious exercises are permitted a "religion of secularism" is established in the schools. We agree of course that the State may not establish a "religion of secularism" in the sense of affirmatively opposing or showing hostility to religion, thus "preferring those who believe in no religion over those who do believe." We do not agree, however, that this decision in any sense has that effect. In addition, it might well be said that one's education is not complete without a study of comparative religion or the history of religion and its relationship to the advancement of civilization. It certainly may be said that the Bible is worthy of study for its literary and historic qualities. Nothing we have said here indicates that such study of the Bible or of religion, when presented objectively as part of a secular program of education, may not be effected consistently with the First Amendment. But the exercise . . . [is a] religious [exercise], required by the [State] in violation of the command of the First Amendment that the Government maintain strict neutrality, neither aiding nor opposing religion.

Finally, we cannot accept that the concept of neutrality, which does not permit a State to require a religious exercise even with the consent of the majority of those affected, collides with the majority's right to free exercise of religion. While the Free Exercise Clause clearly prohibits the use of state action to deny the rights of free exercise to *anyone*, it has never meant that a majority could use the machinery of the State to practice its beliefs. Such a contention was effectively answered by Justice Jackson for the Court in *West Virginia State Board of Education v. Barnett:*

> "The very purpose of a Bill of Rights was to with-draw certain subjects from the vicissitudes of po-litical controversy, to place them beyond the reach of majorities and officials and to establish them as legal principles to be applied by the courts. One's right to . . . freedom of worship . . . and other fundamental rights may not be submitted to vote; they depend on the outcome of no elections."

The place of religion in our society is an exalted one, achieved through a long tradition of reliance on the home, the church and the inviolable citadel of the individual heart and mind. We have come to recognize through bitter expe-rience that it is not within the power of government to in-vade that citadel, whether its purpose or effect be to aid or oppose, to advance or retard. In the relationship between man and religion, the State is firmly committed to a posi-tion of neutrality. Though the application of that rule re-quires interpretation of a delicate sort, the rule itself is clearly and concisely stated in the words of the First Amendment. Applying that rule to [this case], we affirm the judgment. . . .

It is so ordered.

Schoolhouse Speech
Tinker v. Des Moines Schools

A former student had been killed in Vietnam. It was felt that any kind of [anti-war] demonstration might evolve into something difficult to control. - **The Des Moines School District**

On December 16, 1965, John Tinker, 15, and Christopher Eckhardt, Jr., 16, students at a Des Moines, Iowa public high school, wore black armbands to their school as a protest against the war in Vietnam. John Tinker's younger sister, Mary Beth, 13, a student at a Des Moines Public Junior High School, did the same. The Des Moines School District, alerted that the anti-war protest was to be held, adopted, on December 14, this protest ban: Any student wearing a black armband to school would be ordered to remove it, and if they failed to do so, would be suspended. The Tinkers and Eckhardt were informed of the ban but decided to go forward with their schoolhouse protest. Christopher, John, and Mary Beth were all suspended from school until they returned without their armbands.

Their fathers, Leonard Tinker and Christopher Eckhardt, Sr., filed a lawsuit on their behalf in Federal District Court, asking for the protest ban to be lifted and for their children to be allowed to return to school, arguing that the ban was an unconstitutional violation of their First Amendment rights. The District Court upheld the ban as an action that was reasonable to prevent a disturbance of school discipline. The U.S. Court of Appeals affirmed the District Court's decision. The Tinkers and Eckhardts appealed to the U.S. Supreme Court.

Oral arguments were heard in *Tinker v. Des Moines Schools* on November 12, 1968 and on February 24, 1969 the 7-2 decision of the Court was announced by Associate Justice Abe Fortas.

The Tinker Court

Chief Justice Earl Warren
Appointed Chief Justice by President Eisenhower
Served 1953 - 1969

Associate Justice Hugo Black
Appointed by President Franklin Roosevelt
Served 1937 - 1971

Associate Justice William O. Douglas
Appointed by President Franklin Roosevelt
Served 1939 - 1975

Associate Justice John Marshall Harlan
Appointed by President Eisenhower
Served 1955 - 1971

Associate Justice William Brennan
Appointed by President Eisenhower
Served 1956 -1990

Associate Justice Potter Stewart
Appointed by President Eisenhower
Served 1958 - 1981

Associate Justice Byron White
Appointed by President Kennedy
Served 1962 - 1993

Associate Justice Abe Fortas
Appointed by President Lyndon Johnson
Served 1965 - 1969

Associate Justice Thurgood Marshall
Appointed by President Lyndon Johnson
Served 1967 - 1991

The unedited text of *Tinker v. Des Moines Schools* can be found on page 503, volume 393 of *United States Reports*. Our edited text follows.

TINKER v. DES MOINES SCHOOLS
February 24, 1969

JUSTICE ABE FORTAS: Petitioner John F. Tinker, 15 years old, and petitioner Christopher Eckhardt, 16 years old, attended high schools in Des Moines, Iowa. Petitioner Mary Beth Tinker, John's sister, was a 13-year-old student in junior high school.

In December 1965, a group of adults and students in Des Moines held a meeting at the Eckhardt home. The group determined to publicize their objections to the hostilities in Vietnam and their support for a truce by wearing black armbands during the holiday season and by fasting on December 16 and New Year's Eve. [The Tinkers and Eckhardt] and their parents had previously engaged in similar activities, and they decided to participate in the program.

The principals of the Des Moines schools became aware of the plan to wear armbands. On December 14, 1965, they met and adopted a policy that any student wearing an armband to school would be asked to remove it, and if he refused he would be suspended until he returned without the armband. [The Tinkers and Eckhardt] were aware of the regulation that the school authorities adopted.

On December 16, Mary Beth and Christopher wore black armbands to their schools. John Tinker wore his armband the next day. They were all sent home and suspended from school until they would come back without their armbands. They did not return to school until after the planned period for wearing armbands had expired - that is, until after New Year's Day.

This complaint was filed in the United States District Court by [the Tinkers and Eckhardt], through their fathers. . . . It prayed [asked] for an injunction [court order stopping an act] restraining the respondent school officials and the respondent members of the board of directors of the school district from disciplining the [Tinkers and Eckhardt], and it sought nominal damages. After [a] hearing the District Court dismissed the complaint. It upheld the constitutionality of the school authorities' action on the ground that it was reasonable in order to prevent disturbance of school discipline. The court referred to but expressly declined to follow the Fifth Circuit's holding in a similar case that the wearing of symbols like the armbands cannot be prohibited unless it "materially and substantially interfere[s] with the requirements of appropriate discipline in the operation of the school."

On appeal, the Court of Appeals . . . was equally divided, and the District Court's decision was accordingly affirmed [upheld], without opinion. We granted certiorari [agreed to hear the case].

The District Court recognized that the wearing of an armband for the purpose of expressing certain views is the type of symbolic act that is within the Free Speech Clause of the First Amendment. As we shall discuss, the wearing of armbands in the circumstances of this case was entirely divorced from actually or potentially disruptive conduct by those participating in it. It was closely akin to "pure speech" which, we have repeatedly held, is entitled to comprehensive protection under the First Amendment.

First Amendment rights, applied in light of the special characteristics of the school environment, are available to teachers and students. It can hardly be argued that either students or teachers shed their constitutional rights to freedom of speech or expression at the schoolhouse gate. This has been the unmistakable holding of this Court for almost 50 years. In *Meyer v. Nebraska* and *Bartels v. Iowa*, this Court, in opinions by Justice McReynolds, held that the Due Process Clause of the Fourteenth Amendment prevents States from forbidding the teaching of a foreign language to young students. Statutes to this effect, the Court held, unconstitutionally interfere with the liberty of teacher, student, and parent.

In *West Virginia v. Barnette*, this Court held that under the First Amendment, the student in public school may not be compelled to salute the flag. Speaking through Justice Jackson, the Court said:

> "The Fourteenth Amendment, as now applied to the States, protects the citizen against the State itself and all of its creatures - Boards of Education not excepted. These have, of course, important, delicate, and highly discretionary functions, but none that they may not perform within the limits of the Bill of Rights. That they are educating the young for citizenship is reason for scrupulous protection of Constitutional freedoms of the individual, if we are not to strangle the free mind at its source and teach youth to discount important principles of our government as mere platitudes."

On the other hand, the Court has repeatedly emphasized the need for affirming the comprehensive authority of the States and of school officials, consistent with fundamental constitutional safeguards, to prescribe and control conduct in the schools. Our problem lies in the area where students in the exercise of First Amendment rights collide with the rules of the school authorities.

The problem posed by the present case does not relate to regulation of the length of skirts or the type of clothing, to hair style, or deportment. It does not concern aggressive, disruptive action or even group demonstrations. Our problem involves direct, primary First Amendment rights akin to "pure speech."

The school officials banned and sought to punish [the Tinkers and Eckhardt] for a silent, passive expression of opinion, unaccompanied by any disorder or disturbance on [their] part. . . . There is here no evidence whatever of [the Tinkers' and Eckhardt]'s interference, actual or nascent, with the schools' work or of collision with the rights of other students to be secure and to be let alone. Accordingly, this case does not concern speech or action that intrudes upon the work of the schools or the rights of other students.

Only a few of the 18,000 students in the school system wore the black armbands. Only five students were suspended for wearing them. There is no indication that the work of the schools or any class was disrupted. Outside the classrooms, a few students made hostile remarks to the children wearing armbands, but there were no threats or acts of violence on school premises.

The District Court concluded that the action of the school authorities was reasonable because it was based upon their fear of a disturbance from the wearing of the armbands. But, in our system, undifferentiated fear or apprehension of disturbance is not enough to overcome the right to freedom of expression. Any departure from absolute regimentation may cause trouble. Any variation from the majority's opinion may inspire fear. Any word spoken, in class, in the lunchroom, or on the campus, that deviates from the views of another person may start an argument or cause a disturbance. But our Constitution says we must take this risk; and our history says that it is this sort of hazardous freedom - this kind of openness - that is the basis of our national strength and of the independence and vigor of Americans who grow up and live in this relatively permissive, often disputatious, society.

In order for the State in the person of school officials to justify prohibition of a particular expression of opinion, it must be able to show that its action was caused by something more than a mere desire to avoid the discomfort and unpleasantness that always accompany an unpopular viewpoint. Certainly where there is no finding and no showing that engaging in of the forbidden conduct would "materially and substantially interfere with the requirements of appropriate discipline in the operation of the school," the prohibition cannot be sustained [upheld].

In the present case, the District Court made no such finding, and our independent examination of the record fails to yield evidence that the school authorities had reason to anticipate that the wearing of the armbands would substantially interfere with the work of the school or impinge upon the rights of other students. Even an official memorandum prepared after the suspension that listed the reasons for the ban on wearing the armbands made no reference to the anticipation of such disruption.

On the contrary, the action of the school authorities appears to have been based upon an urgent wish to avoid the controversy which might result from the expression, even by the silent symbol of armbands, of opposition to this Nation's part in the conflagration in Vietnam. It is revealing, in this respect, that the meeting at which the school principals decided to issue the contested regulation was called in response to a student's statement to the journalism teacher in one of the schools that he wanted to write an article on Vietnam and have it published in the school paper. (The student was dissuaded.)

It is also relevant that the school authorities did not purport to prohibit the wearing of all symbols of political or controversial significance. The record shows that students in some of the schools wore buttons relating to national political campaigns, and some even wore the Iron Cross, traditionally a symbol of Nazism. The order prohibiting the wearing of armbands did not extend to these. Instead, a particular symbol - black armbands worn to exhibit opposition to this Nation's involvement in Vietnam - was singled out for prohibition. Clearly, the prohibition of expression of one particular opinion, at least without evidence that it is necessary to avoid material and substantial interference with schoolwork or discipline, is not constitutionally permissible.

In our system, state-operated schools may not be enclaves of totalitarianism. School officials do not possess absolute authority over their students. Students in school as well as out of school are "persons" under our Constitution. They are possessed of fundamental rights which the State must respect, just as they themselves must respect their obligations to the State. In our system, students may not be regarded as closed-circuit recipients of only that which the State chooses to communicate. They may not be confined to the expression of those sentiments that are officially approved. In the absence of a specific showing of constitutionally valid reasons to regulate their speech, students are entitled to freedom of expression of their views. As Judge Gewin, speaking for the Fifth Circuit, said, school officials cannot suppress "expressions of feelings with which they do not wish to contend."

In *Meyer v. Nebraska,* Justice McReynolds expressed this Nation's repudiation of the principle that a State might so conduct its schools as to "foster a homogeneous people." He said:

> "In order to submerge the individual and develop ideal citizens, Sparta assembled the males at seven into barracks and intrusted their subsequent education and training to official guardians. Although such measures have been deliberately approved by men of great genius, their ideas touching the relation between individual and State were wholly different from those upon which our institutions rest; and it hardly will be affirmed that any legislature could impose such restrictions upon the people of a State without doing violence to both letter and spirit of the Constitution."

This principle has been repeated by this Court on numerous occasions during the intervening years. In *Keyishian v. Board of Regents*, Justice Brennan, speaking for the Court, said:

> "'The vigilant protection of constitutional freedoms is nowhere more vital than in the community of American schools.' The classroom is peculiarly the 'market place of ideas.' The Nation's future depends upon leaders trained through wide exposure to that robust exchange of ideas which discovers truth 'out of a multitude of tongues, [rather] than through any kind of authoritative selection.'"

The principle of these cases is not confined to the supervised and ordained discussion which takes place in the classroom. The principal use to which the schools are dedicated is to accommodate students during prescribed hours for the purpose of certain types of activities. Among those activities is personal intercommunication among the students. This is not only an inevitable part of the process of attending school; it is also an important part of the educational process. A student's rights, therefore, do not embrace merely the classroom hours. When he is in the cafeteria, or on the playing field, or on the campus during the authorized hours, he may express his opinions, even on controversial subjects like the conflict in Vietnam, if he does so without "materially and substantially interfer[ing] with the requirements of appropriate discipline in the operation of the school" and without colliding with the rights of others. But conduct by the student, in class or out of it, which for any reason - whether it stems from time, place, or type of behavior - materially disrupts classwork or involves substantial disorder or invasion of the rights of others is, of course, not immunized by the constitutional guarantee of freedom of speech.

Under our Constitution, free speech is not a right that is given only to be so circumscribed that it exists in principle but not in fact. Freedom of expression would not truly exist if the right could be exercised only in an area that a benevolent government has provided as a safe haven for crackpots. The Constitution says that Congress (and the States) may not abridge the right to free speech. This provision means what it says. We properly read it to permit reasonable regulation of speech-connected activities in carefully restricted circumstances. But we do not confine the permissible exercise of First Amendment rights to a telephone booth or the four corners of a pamphlet, or to supervised and ordained discussion in a school classroom.

If a regulation were adopted by school officials forbidding discussion of the Vietnam conflict, or the expression by any student of opposition to it anywhere on school property except as part of a prescribed classroom exercise, it would be obvious that the regulation would violate the constitutional rights of students, at least if it could not be justified by a showing that the students' activities would materially and substantially disrupt the work and discipline of the school. In the circumstances of the present case, the prohibition of the silent, passive "witness of the armbands," as one of the children called it, is no less offensive to the Constitution's guarantees.

As we have discussed, the record does not demonstrate any facts which might reasonably have led school authorities to forecast substantial disruption of or material interference with school activities, and no disturbances or disorders on the school premises in fact occurred. [The Tinkers and Eckhardt] merely went about their ordained rounds in school. Their deviation consisted only in wearing on their sleeve a band of black cloth, not more than two inches wide. They wore it to exhibit their disapproval of the Vietnam hostilities and their advocacy of a truce, to make their views known, and, by their example, to influence others to adopt them. They neither interrupted school activities nor sought to intrude in the school affairs or the lives of others. They caused discussion outside of the class rooms, but no interference with work and no disorder. In the circumstances, our Constitution does not permit officials of the State to deny their form of expression.

We express no opinion as to the form of relief which should be granted, this being a matter for the lower courts to determine. We reverse and remand [send back to the lower court] for further proceedings consistent with this opinion.

Corporal Punishment
Ingraham v. Wright

Corporal Punishment: *The moderate use of physical force or physical contact by a teacher or principal as may be necessary to maintain discipline or to enforce school rules.*

During the 1970-1971 school year at Dade County, Florida's Drew Junior High School, James Ingraham, an eighth grader, and Roosevelt Andrews, a ninth grader, were subjected to state-sanctioned corporal punishment inflicted with a wooden paddle. Ingraham, paddled for being slow to respond, took eleven days to recover. Andrews, paddled for minor infractions, lost the use of his arm for a week.

Eloise Ingraham, the mother of James, and Willie Everett, the father of Roosevelt, sued school officials, including Drew Junior High's Principal, Willie Wright, to halt the paddlings. The parents, on behalf of their minor children, argued that the infliction of corporal punishment in the public schools as a means to enforce discipline was a violation of their children's Eight Amendment protection against cruel and unusual punishment. They also argued that the infliction of such punishment without prior notice and a hearing was a violation of their children's Fourteenth Amendment Due Process rights.

The United States District Court held that the punishments authorized by the state and used by school officials on Ingraham and Andrews did not, in their case, violate the Constitution. The students appealed. The United States Court of Appeals upheld the District Court. Ingraham and Andrews appealed to the United States Supreme Court.

Oral arguments were heard on November 2-3, 1976 and the 5-4 decision of the Court was announced on April 19, 1977 by Associate Justice Lewis Powell.

The Ingraham Court

Chief Justice Warren Burger
Appointed Chief Justice by President Nixon
Served 1969 - 1986

Associate Justice William Brennan
Appointed by President Eisenhower
Served 1956 - 1990

Associate Justice Potter Stewart
Appointed by President Eisenhower
Served 1958 - 1981

Associate Justice Byron White
Appointed by President Kennedy
Served 1962 - 1993

Associate Justice Thurgood Marshall
Appointed by President Johnson
Served 1967 - 1991

Associate Justice Harry Blackmun
Appointed by President Nixon
Served 1970 - 1994

Associate Justice Lewis Powell
Appointed by President Nixon
Served 1971 - 1987

Associate Justice William Rehnquist
Appointed by President Nixon
Served 1971 -

Associate Justice John Paul Stevens
Appointed by President Ford
Served 1975 -

The unedited text of *Ingraham v. Wright* can be found on page 651, volume 430 of *United States Reports*. Our edited text follows.

INGRAHAM v. WRIGHT
April 19, 1977

JUSTICE LEWIS POWELL: This case presents questions concerning the use of corporal punishment in public schools: First, whether the paddling of students as a means of maintaining school discipline constitutes cruel and unusual punishment in violation of the Eighth Amendment; and, second, to the extent that paddling is constitutionally permissible, whether the Due Process Clause of the Fourteenth Amendment requires prior notice and an opportunity to be heard.

Petitioners James Ingraham and Roosevelt Andrews filed the complaint in this case on January 7, 1971, in the United States District Court for the Southern District of Florida. At the time both were enrolled in the Charles R. Drew Junior High School in Dade County, Florida, Ingraham in the eighth grade and Andrews in the ninth. The complaint contained three counts, each alleging . . . deprivation of constitutional rights. . . . Counts one and two were individual actions for damages by Ingraham and Andrews based on paddling incidents that allegedly occurred in October 1970 at Drew Junior High School. Count three was a class action . . . filed on behalf of all students in the Dade County schools. Named as defendants in all counts were respondents Willie J. Wright (principal at Drew Junior High School), Lemmie Deliford (an assistant principal), Solomon Barnes (an assistant to the principal), and Edward L. Whigham (superintendent of the Dade County School System).

[Ingraham] presented . . . evidence at a week-long trial before the District Court. At the close of [his] case, [Wright] moved for dismissal of count three . . . and for a ruling that the evidence would be insufficient to go to a jury on counts one and two. The District Court granted the motion as to all three counts, and dismissed the complaint without hearing evidence on behalf of the school authorities.

[Ingraham's] evidence may be summarized briefly. In the 1970-1971 school year many of the 237 schools in Dade County used corporal punishment as a means of maintaining discipline pursuant to Florida legislation and a local School Board regulation. The statute then in effect authorized limited corporal punishment by negative inference, proscribing punishment which was "degrading or unduly severe" or which was inflicted without prior consultation with the principal or the teacher in charge of the school. The regulation, Dade County School Board Policy 5144, contained explicit directions and limitations. The authorized punishment consisted of paddling the recalcitrant student on the buttocks with a flat wooden paddle measuring less than two feet long, three to four inches wide, and about one-half inch thick. The normal punishment was limited to one to five "licks" or blows with the paddle and resulted in no apparent physical injury to the student. School authorities viewed corporal punishment as a less drastic means of discipline than suspension or expulsion. Contrary to the procedural requirements of the statute and regulation, teachers often paddled students on their own authority without first consulting the principal.

[The focus was] on Drew Junior High School, the school in which both Ingraham and Andrews were enrolled in the fall of 1970. In an apparent reference to Drew, the District Court found that "[t]he instances of punishment which could be characterized as severe, accepting the students' testimony as credible, took place in one junior high school." The evidence, consisting mainly of the testimony of 16 students, suggests that the regime at Drew was exceptionally harsh. The testimony of Ingraham and Andrews, in support of their individual claims for damages, is illustrative. Because he was slow to respond to his teacher's instructions, Ingraham was subjected to more than 20 licks with a paddle while being held over a table in the principal's office. The paddling was so severe that he suffered a hematoma requiring medical attention and keeping him out of school for several days. Andrews was paddled several times for minor infractions. On two occasions he was struck on his arms, once depriving him of the full use of his arm for a week.

The District Court made no findings on the credibility of the students' testimony. Rather, assuming their testimony to be credible, the court found no constitutional basis for relief. With respect to count three, the class action, the court concluded that the punishment authorized and practiced generally in the county schools violated no constitutional right. With respect to counts one and two, . . . the court concluded that while corporal punishment could in some cases violate the Eighth Amendment, in this case a jury could not lawfully find "the elements of severity, arbitrary infliction, unacceptability in terms of contemporary standards, or gross disproportion which are necessary to bring 'punishment' to the constitutional level of 'cruel and unusual punishment.'"

A panel of the Court of Appeals voted to reverse. The panel concluded that the punishment was so severe and oppressive as to violate the Eighth and Fourteenth Amendments, and that the procedures outlined in Policy 5144 failed to satisfy the requirements of the Due Process Clause. Upon rehearing, the en banc court [with the entire court participating in the decision] rejected these conclusions and affirmed [upheld] the judgment of the District

Court. The full court held that the Due Process Clause did not require notice or an opportunity to be heard:

> "In essence, we refuse to set forth, as constitutionally mandated, procedural standards for an activity which is not substantial enough, on a constitutional level, to justify the time and effort which would have to be expended by the school in adhering to those procedures or to justify further interference by federal courts into the internal affairs of public schools."

. . . . The Eighth Amendment, in the court's view, was simply inapplicable to corporal punishment in public schools. Stressing the likelihood of civil and criminal liability in state law, if [Ingraham's] evidence [was] believed, the court held that "[t]he administration of corporal punishment in public schools, whether or not excessively administered, does not come within the scope of Eighth Amendment protection." Nor was there any substantive violation of the Due Process Clause. The court noted that "[p]addling of recalcitrant children has long been an accepted method of promoting good behavior and instilling notions of responsibility and decorum into the mischievous heads of school children." The court refused to examine instances of punishment individually:

> "We think it a misuse of our judicial power to determine, for example, whether a teacher has acted arbitrarily in paddling a particular child for certain behavior or whether in a particular instance of misconduct five licks would have been a more appropriate punishment than ten licks. . . ."

We granted certiorari [agreed to hear the case], limited to the questions of cruel and unusual punishment and procedural due process.

In addressing the scope of the Eighth Amendment's prohibition on cruel and unusual punishment, this Court has found it useful to refer to "[t]raditional common-law [law established by custom and usage] concepts," and to the "attitude[s] which our society has traditionally taken." So, too, in defining the requirements of procedural due process under the Fifth and Fourteenth Amendments, the Court has been attuned to what "has always been the law of the land," and to "traditional ideas of fair procedure." We therefore begin by examining the way in which our traditions and our laws have responded to the use of corporal punishment in public schools.

The use of corporal punishment in this country as a means of disciplining schoolchildren dates back to the colonial period. It has survived the transformation of primary and secondary education from the colonials' reliance on optional private arrangements to our present system of compulsory education and dependence on public schools. Despite the general abandonment of corporal punishment as a means of punishing criminal offenders, the practice continues to play a role in the public education of schoolchildren in most parts of the country. Professional and public opinion is sharply divided on the practice, and has been for more than a century. Yet we can discern no trend toward its elimination.

At common law a single principle has governed the use of corporal punishment since before the American Revolution: Teachers may impose reasonable but not excessive force to discipline a child. Blackstone catalogued among the "absolute rights of individuals" the right "to security from the corporal insults of menaces, assaults, beating, and wounding," but he did not regard it a "corporal insult" for a teacher to inflict "moderate correction" on a child in his care. To the extent that force was "necessary to answer the purposes for which [the teacher] is employed," Blackstone viewed it as "justifiable or lawful." The basic doctrine has not changed. The prevalent rule in this country today privileges such force as a teacher or administrator "reasonably believes to be necessary for [the child's] proper control, training, or education." To the extent that the force is excessive or unreasonable, the educator in virtually all States is subject to possible civil and criminal liability.

Although the early cases viewed the authority of the teacher as deriving from the parents, the concept of parental delegation has been replaced by the view - more consonant with compulsory education laws - that the State itself may impose such corporal punishment as is reasonably necessary "for the proper education of the child and for the maintenance of group discipline." All of the circumstances are to be taken into account in determining whether the punishment is reasonable in a particular case. Among the most important considerations are the seriousness of the offense, the attitude and past behavior of the child, the nature and severity of the punishment, the age and strength of the child, and the availability of less severe but equally effective means of discipline.

Of the 23 States that have addressed the problem through legislation, 21 have authorized the moderate use of corporal punishment in public schools. Of these States only a few have elaborated on the common-law test of reasonableness, typically providing for approval or notification of the child's parents, or for infliction of punishment only by the principal or in the presence of an adult witness. Only two States, Massachusetts and New Jersey, have prohibited all corporal punishment in their public schools. Where the legislatures have not acted, the state courts have uniformly preserved the common-law rule permitting teachers to use reasonable force in disciplining children in their charge.

Against this background of historical and contemporary approval of reasonable corporal punishment, we turn to the constitutional questions before us.

The Eighth Amendment provides: "Excessive bail shall not be required, nor excessive fines imposed, nor cruel and unusual punishments inflicted." Bail, fines, and punishment traditionally have been associated with the criminal process, and by subjecting the three to parallel limitations the text of the Amendment suggests an intention to limit the power of those entrusted with the criminal-law function of government. An examination of the history of the Amendment and the decisions of this Court construing [interpreting] the proscription against cruel and unusual punishment confirms that it was designed to protect those convicted of crimes. We adhere to this long-standing limitation and hold that the Eighth Amendment does not apply to the paddling of children as a means of maintaining discipline in public schools.

The history of the Eighth Amendment is well known. The text was taken, almost verbatim, from a provision of the Virginia Declaration of Rights of 1776, which in turn derived from the English Bill of Rights of 1689. The English version, adopted after the accession of William and Mary, was intended to curb the excesses of English judges under the reign of James II. Historians have viewed the English provision as a reaction either to the "Bloody Assize," the treason trials conducted by Chief Justice Jeffreys in 1685 after the abortive rebellion of the Duke of Monmouth, or to the perjury prosecution of Titus Oates in the same year. In either case, the exclusive concern of the English version was the conduct of judges in enforcing the criminal law. The original draft introduced in the House of Commons provided:

> "The requiring excessive bail of persons committed in criminal cases and imposing excessive fines, and illegal punishments, to be prevented."

Although the reference to "criminal cases" was eliminated from the final draft, the preservation of a similar reference in the preamble indicates that the deletion was without substantive significance. Thus, Blackstone treated each of the provision's three prohibitions as bearing only on criminal proceedings and judgments.

The Americans who adopted the language of this part of the English Bill of Rights in framing their own State and Federal Constitutions 100 years later feared the imposition of torture and other cruel punishments not only by judges acting beyond their lawful authority, but also by legislatures engaged in making the laws by which judicial authority would be measured. Indeed, the principal concern of the American Framers appears to have been with the legislative definition of crimes and punishments. But if the American provision was intended to restrain government more broadly than its English model, the subject to which it was intended to apply - the criminal process - was the same.

At the time of its ratification, the original Constitution was criticized in the Massachusetts and Virginia Conventions for its failure to provide any protection for persons convicted of crimes. This criticism provided the impetus for inclusion of the Eighth Amendment in the Bill of Rights. When the Eighth Amendment was debated in the First Congress, it was met by the objection that the Cruel and Unusual Punishments Clause might have the effect of outlawing what were then the common criminal punishments of hanging, whipping, and earcropping. The objection was not heeded, "precisely because the legislature would otherwise have had the unfettered power to prescribe punishments for crimes."

In light of this history, it is not surprising to find that every decision of this Court considering whether a punishment is "cruel and unusual" within the meaning of the Eighth and Fourteenth Amendments has dealt with a criminal punishment.

These decisions recognize that the Cruel and Unusual Punishments Clause circumscribes the criminal process in three ways: First, it limits the kinds of punishment that can be imposed on those convicted of crimes; second, it proscribes punishment grossly disproportionate to the severity of the crime; and third, it imposes substantive limits on what can be made criminal and punished as such. We have recognized the last limitation as one to be applied sparingly. "The primary purpose of [the Cruel and Unusual Punishments Clause] has always been considered, and properly so, to be directed at the method or kind of punishment imposed for the violation of criminal statutes. . . ."

In the few cases where the Court has had occasion to confront claims that impositions outside the criminal process constituted cruel and unusual punishment, it has had no difficulty finding the Eighth Amendment inapplicable. . . .

[Ingraham] acknowledge[s] that the original design of the Cruel and Unusual Punishments Clause was to limit criminal punishments, but urge nonetheless that the prohibition should be extended to ban the paddling of schoolchildren. Observing that the Framers of the Eighth Amendment could not have envisioned our present system of public and compulsory education, with its opportunities for noncriminal punishments, [Ingraham] contend[s] that extension of the prohibition against cruel punishments is necessary lest we afford greater protection to criminals than to schoolchildren. It would be anomalous, they say, if schoolchildren could be beaten without constitutional redress, while hardened criminals suffering the same beatings at the hands of their jailers might have a valid claim under the Eighth Amendment. Whatever force this logic may have in other settings, we find it an inadequate basis for wrenching the Eighth Amendment from its historical context and extending it to traditional disciplinary practices in the public schools.

The prisoner and the schoolchild stand in wholly different circumstances, separated by the harsh facts of criminal conviction and incarceration. The prisoner's conviction entitles the State to classify him as a "criminal," and his incarceration deprives him of the freedom "to be with family and friends and to form the other enduring attachments of normal life." Prison brutality, as the Court of Appeals observed in this case, is "part of the total punishment to which the individual is being subjected for his crime and, as such, is a proper subject for Eighth Amendment scrutiny." Even so, the protection afforded by the Eighth Amendment is limited. After incarceration, only the "'unnecessary and wanton infliction of pain'" constitutes cruel and unusual punishment forbidden by the Eighth Amendment.

The schoolchild has little need for the protection of the Eighth Amendment. Though attendance may not always be voluntary, the public school remains an open institution. Except perhaps when very young, the child is not physically restrained from leaving school during school hours; and at the end of the school day, the child is invariably free to return home. Even while at school, the child brings with him the support of family and friends and is rarely apart from teachers and other pupils who may witness and protest any instances of mistreatment.

The openness of the public school and its supervision by the community afford significant safeguards against the kinds of abuses from which the Eighth Amendment protects the prisoner. In virtually every community where corporal punishment is permitted in the schools, these safeguards are reinforced by the legal constraints of the common law. Public school teachers and administrators are privileged at common law to inflict only such corporal punishment as is reasonably necessary for the proper education and discipline of the child; any punishment going beyond the privilege may result in both civil and criminal liability. As long as the schools are open to public scrutiny, there is no reason to believe that the common-law constraints will not effectively remedy and deter excesses such as those alleged in this case.

We conclude that when public school teachers or administrators impose disciplinary corporal punishment, the Eighth Amendment is inapplicable. The pertinent constitutional question is whether the imposition is consonant with the requirements of due process.

The Fourteenth Amendment prohibits any state deprivation of life, liberty, or property without due process of law. Application of this prohibition requires the familiar two-stage analysis: We must first ask whether the asserted individual interests are encompassed within the Fourteenth Amendment's protection of "life, liberty or property"; if protected interests are implicated, we then must decide what procedures constitute "due process of law." Following that analysis here, we find that corporal punishment in public schools implicates a constitutionally protected liberty interest, but we hold that the traditional common-law remedies are fully adequate to afford due process.

"[T]he range of interests protected by procedural due process is not infinite." We have repeatedly rejected "the notion that *any* grievous loss visited upon a person by the State is sufficient to invoke the procedural protections of the Due Process Clause." Due process is required only when a decision of the State implicates an interest within the protection of the Fourteenth Amendment. And "to determine whether due process requirements apply in the first place, we must look not to the 'weight' but to the *nature* of the interest at stake."

The Due Process Clause of the Fifth Amendment, later incorporated into the Fourteenth, was intended to give Americans at least the protection against governmental power that they had enjoyed as Englishmen against the power of the Crown. The liberty preserved from deprivation without due process included the right "generally to enjoy those privileges long recognized at common law as essential to the orderly pursuit of happiness by free men." Among the historic liberties so protected was a right to be free from, and to obtain judicial relief for, unjustified intrusions on personal security.

While the contours of this historic liberty interest in the context of our federal system of government have not been defined precisely, they always have been thought to encompass freedom from bodily restraint and punishment. It is fundamental that the state cannot hold and physically punish an individual except in accordance with due process of law.

This constitutionally protected liberty interest is at stake in this case. There is, of course, a de minimis [insignificant] level of imposition with which the Constitution is not concerned. But at least where school authorities, acting under color of state law, deliberately decide to punish a child for misconduct by restraining the child and inflicting appreciable physical pain, we hold that Fourteenth Amendment liberty interests are implicated.

"[T]he question remains what process is due." Were it not for the common-law privilege permitting teachers to inflict reasonable corporal punishment on children in their care, and the availability of the traditional remedies for abuse, the case for requiring advance procedural safeguards would be strong indeed. But here we deal with a punishment - paddling - within that tradition, and the question is whether the common-law remedies are adequate to afford due process.

> "'[D]ue process,' unlike some legal rules, is not a technical conception with a fixed content unrelated to time, place and circumstances. . . . Representing a profound attitude of fairness . . . 'due process' is compounded of history, reason, the past course of decisions, and stout confidence in the strength of the democratic faith which we profess. . . ."

Whether in this case the common-law remedies for excessive corporal punishment constitute due process of law must turn on an analysis of the competing interests at stake, viewed against the background of "history, reason, [and] the past course of decisions." The analysis requires consideration of three distinct factors: "First, the private interest that will be affected . . .; second, the risk of an erroneous deprivation of such interest . . . and the probable value, if any, of additional or substitute procedural safeguards; and finally, the [state] interest, including the function involved and the fiscal and administrative burdens that the additional or substitute procedural requirement would entail."

Because it is rooted in history, the child's liberty interest in avoiding corporal punishment while in the care of public school authorities is subject to historical limitations. Under the common law, an invasion of personal security gave rise to a right to recover damages in a subsequent judicial proceeding. But the right of recovery was qualified by the concept of justification. Thus, there could be no recovery against a teacher who gave only "moderate correction" to a child. To the extent that the force used was reasonable in light of its purpose, it was not wrongful, but rather "justifiable or lawful."

The concept that reasonable corporal punishment in school is justifiable continues to be recognized in the laws of most States. It represents "the balance struck by this country" between the child's interest in personal security and the traditional view that some limited corporal punishment may be necessary in the course of a child's education. Under that longstanding accommodation of interests, there can be no deprivation of substantive rights as long as disciplinary corporal punishment is within the limits of the common-law privilege.

This is not to say that the child's interest in procedural safeguards is insubstantial. The school disciplinary process is not "a totally accurate, unerring process, never mistaken and never unfair. . . ." In any deliberate infliction of corporal punishment on a child who is restrained for that purpose, there is some risk that the intrusion on the child's liberty will be unjustified and therefore unlawful. In these circumstances the child has a strong interest in procedural safeguards that minimize the risk of wrongful punishment and provide for the resolution of disputed questions of justification.

We turn now to a consideration of the safeguards that are available under applicable Florida law.

Florida has continued to recognize, and indeed has strengthened by statute, the common-law right of a child not to be subjected to excessive corporal punishment in school. Under Florida law the teacher and principal of the school decide in the first instance whether corporal punishment is reasonably necessary under the circumstances in order to discipline a child who has misbehaved. But they must exercise prudence and restraint. For Florida has preserved the traditional judicial proceedings for determining whether the punishment was justified. If the punishment inflicted is later found to have been excessive - not reasonably believed at the time to be necessary for the child's discipline or training - the school authorities inflicting it may be held liable in damages to the child and, if malice is shown, they may be subject to criminal penalties.

Although students have testified in this case to specific instances of abuse, there is every reason to believe that such mistreatment is an aberration. The uncontradicted evidence suggests that corporal punishment in the Dade County schools was, "[w]ith the exception of a few cases, . . . unremarkable in physical severity." Moreover, because paddlings are usually inflicted in response to conduct directly observed by teachers in their presence, the risk that a child will be paddled without cause is typically insignificant. In the ordinary case, a disciplinary paddling neither threatens seriously to violate any substantive rights nor condemns the child "to suffer grievous loss of any kind."

In those cases where severe punishment is contemplated, the available civil and criminal sanctions for abuse - considered in light of the openness of the school environment - afford significant protection against unjustified corporal punishment. Teachers and school authorities are unlikely to inflict corporal punishment unnecessarily or excessively when a possible consequence of doing so is the institution of civil or criminal proceedings against them.

It still may be argued, of course, that the child's liberty interest would be better protected if the common-law remedies were supplemented by the administrative safeguards of prior notice and a hearing. We have found frequently that some kind of prior hearing is necessary to guard against arbitrary impositions on interests protected by the Fourteenth Amendment. But where the State has preserved what "has always been the law of the land," the case for administrative safeguards is significantly less compelling.

There is a relevant analogy in the criminal law. Although the Fourth Amendment specifically proscribes "seizure" of a person without probable cause, the risk that police will act unreasonably in arresting a suspect is not thought to require an advance determination of the facts. In *United States v. Watson*, we reaffirmed the traditional common-law rule that police officers may make warrantless public arrests on probable cause. Although we observed that an advance determination of probable cause by a magistrate would be desirable, we declined "to transform this judicial preference into a constitutional rule when the judgment of the Nation and Congress has for so long been to authorize warrantless public arrests on probable cause. . . ." Despite the distinct possibility that a police officer may improperly assess the facts and thus unconstitutionally deprive an individual of liberty, we declined to depart from the traditional rule by which the officer's perception is subjected to judicial scrutiny only after the fact. There is no more reason to depart from tradition and require advance procedural safeguards for intrusions on personal security to which the Fourth Amendment does not apply.

But even if the need for advance procedural safeguards were clear, the question would remain whether the incremental benefit could justify the cost. Acceptance of [Ingraham's] claims would work a transformation in the law governing corporal punishment in Florida and most other States. Given the impracticability of formulating a rule of procedural due process that varies with the severity of the particular imposition, the prior hearing [Ingraham] seek[s] would have to precede *any* paddling, however moderate or trivial.

Such a universal constitutional requirement would significantly burden the use of corporal punishment as a disciplinary measure. Hearings - even informal hearings - require time, personnel, and a diversion of attention from normal school pursuits. School authorities may well choose to abandon corporal punishment rather than incur the burdens of complying with the procedural requirements. Teachers, properly concerned with maintaining authority in the classroom, may well prefer to rely on other disciplinary measures - which they may view as less effective - rather than confront the possible disruption that prior notice and a hearing may entail. Paradoxically, such an alteration of disciplinary policy is most likely to occur in the ordinary case where the contemplated punishment is well within the common-law privilege.

Elimination or curtailment of corporal punishment would be welcomed by many as a societal advance. But when such a policy choice may result from this Court's determination of an asserted right to due process, rather than from the normal processes of community debate and legislative action, the societal costs cannot be dismissed as insubstantial. We are reviewing here a legislative judgment, rooted in history and reaffirmed in the laws of many States, that corporal punishment serves important educational interests. This judgment must be viewed in light of the disciplinary problems commonplace in the schools. As noted in *Goss v. Lopez:* "Events calling for discipline are frequent occurrences and sometimes require immediate, effective action." Assessment of the need for, and the appropriate means of maintaining, school discipline is committed generally to the discretion of school authorities subject to state law. "[T]he Court has repeatedly emphasized the need for affirming the comprehensive authority of the States and of school officials, consistent with fundamental constitutional safeguards, to prescribe and control conduct in the schools."

"At some point the benefit of an additional safeguard to the individual affected . . . and to society in terms of increased assurance that the action is just, may be outweighed by the cost." We think that point has been reached in this case. In view of the low incidence of abuse, the openness of our schools, and the common-law safeguards that already exist, the risk of error that may result in violation of a schoolchild's substantive rights can only be regarded as minimal. Imposing additional administrative safeguards as a constitutional requirement might reduce that risk marginally, but would also entail a significant intrusion into an area of primary educational responsibility. We conclude that the Due Process Clause does not require notice and a hearing prior to the imposition of corporal punishment in the public schools, as that practice is authorized and limited by the common law.

[Ingraham] cannot prevail on either of the theories before us in this case. The Eighth Amendment's prohibition against cruel and unusual punishment is inapplicable to school paddlings, and the Fourteenth Amendment's requirement of procedural due process is satisfied by Florida's preservation of common-law constraints and remedies. We therefore agree with the Court of Appeals that [Ingraham's] evidence affords no basis for . . . relief, and that [he] cannot recover damages on the basis of any Eighth Amendment or procedural due process violation.

Affirmed.

Banning School Library Books
Island Trees Schools v. Pico

*Only by taking a hard look at the way in which we have origi-
nated and then by studying the biological aspects of the way we
behave as a species today, can we really acquire a balanced, objective understanding of our extraordinary existence.*

- Desmond Morris, *The Naked Ape*

In February 1976 Long Island, New York's Island Trees
School Board banned from their junior and senior high
school libraries books that its members believed to be
"anti-American, anti-Christian, vulgar, immoral, and just
plain filthy." The School Board stated: *[It] is our duty, our
moral obligation, to protect the children in our schools from this moral
danger as surely as from physical and medical dangers.*

The books banned from the school library were Vonnegut's *Slaughterhouse Five*, Morris' *Naked Ape*, Thomas'
Down These Mean Streets, Wright's *Black Boy*, Cleaver's *Soul
On Ice*, LaFarge's *Laughing Boy*, Childress' *A Hero Ain't
Nothin' But A Sandwich*, *The Best Short Stories Of Negro Writers*
(an anthology edited by Langston Hughes), and the
anonymously-written *Go Ask Alice*.

Steven Pico, an Island Trees student, sued the School
Board in Federal Court, claiming a violation of his First
Amendment rights. Pico demanded that the School Board
return the banned books to the library. The United States
District Court found for the School Board. The United
States Court of Appeals found for Pico. The School Board
appealed to the United States Supreme Court.

Oral arguments were heard in *Island Trees Schools v. Pico* on
March 2, 1982 and on June 25, 1982 the 5-4 decision of the
Court was announced by Associate Justice William Bren-
nan.

The Island Trees Court

Chief Justice Warren Burger
Appointed Chief Justice by President Nixon
Served 1969 - 1986

Associate Justice William Brennan
Appointed by President Eisenhower
Served 1956 -1990

Associate Justice Byron White
Appointed by President Kennedy
Served 1962 - 1993

Associate Justice Thurgood Marshall
Appointed by President Lyndon Johnson
Served 1967 - 1991

Associate Justice Harry Blackmun
Appointed by President Nixon
Served 1970 - 1994

Associate Justice Lewis Powell
Appointed by President Nixon
Served 1971 - 1987

Associate Justice William Rehnquist
Appointed by President Nixon
Served 1971 -

Associate Justice John Paul Stevens
Appointed by President Ford
Served 1975 -

Associate Justice Sandra Day O'Connor
Appointed by President Reagan
Served 1981 -

The unedited text of *Island Trees Schools v. Pico* can be found on page 853, volume 457 of *United States Reports*. Our edited text follows.

ISLAND TREES SCHOOLS v. PICO
June 25, 1982

JUSTICE WILLIAM BRENNAN: The principal question presented is whether the First Amendment imposes limitations upon the exercise by a local school board of its discretion to remove library books from high school and junior high school libraries.

Petitioners are the Board of Education of the Island Trees Union Free School District No. 26, in New York, and . . . [Richard Ahrens,] the President of the Board, . . . [Frank Martin,] the Vice President, and . . . [other] Board members. The Board is a state agency charged with responsibility for the operation and administration of the public schools within the Island Trees School District. . . . Respondents are Steven Pico, Jacqueline Gold, Glenn Yarris, Russell Rieger, and Paul Sochinski . . . , students at the High School, and . . . Junior High School.

In September 1975, petitioners Ahrens, Martin, and [other School Board members] attended a conference sponsored by Parents of New York United (PONYU), a politically conservative organization of parents concerned about education legislation in the State of New York. At the conference these petitioners obtained lists of books described by Ahrens as "objectionable," and by Martin as "improper fare for school students." It was later determined that the High School library contained nine of the listed books [*Slaughter House Five, The Naked Ape, Down These Mean Streets, Best Short Stories of Negro Writers, Go Ask Alice, Laughing Boy, Black Boy, A Hero Ain't Nothin' But a Sandwich, and Soul on Ice*], and that another listed book [*A Reader for Writers*] was in the Junior High School library. In February 1976, at a meeting with the Superintendent of Schools and the Principals of the

High School and Junior High School, the Board gave an "unofficial direction" that the listed books be removed from the library shelves and delivered to the Board's offices, so that Board members could read them. When this directive was carried out, it became publicized, and the Board issued a press release justifying its action. It characterized the removed books as "anti-American, anti-Christian, anti-Semitic, and just plain filthy," and concluded that "[i]t is our duty, our moral obligation, to protect the children in our schools from this moral danger as surely as from physical and medical dangers."

A short time later, the Board appointed a "Book Review Committee," consisting of four Island Trees parents and four members of the Island Trees schools staff, to read the listed books and to recommend to the Board whether the books should be retained, taking into account the books' "educational suitability," "good taste," "relevance," and "appropriateness to age and grade level." In July, the Committee made its final report to the Board, recommending that five of the listed books be retained and that two others be removed from the school libraries. As for the remaining four books, the Committee could not agree on two, took no position on one, and recommended that the last book be made available to students only with parental approval. The Board substantially rejected the Committee's report later that month, deciding that only one book should be returned to the High School library without restriction, that another should be made available subject to parental approval, but that the remaining nine books should "be removed from elementary and secondary libraries and [from] use in the curriculum." The Board gave no reasons for rejecting the recommendations of the Committee that it had appointed.

Respondents reacted to the Board's decision by bringing the present action. They alleged that petitioners had

> "ordered the removal of the books from school libraries and proscribed [prohibited] their use in the curriculum because particular passages in the books offended their social, political and moral tastes and not because the books, taken as a whole, were lacking in educational value."

[Pico and his fellow students] claimed that the Board's actions denied them their rights under the First Amendment. They asked the court for a declaration that the Board's actions were unconstitutional, and for [the court to order] the Board to return the nine books to the school libraries and to refrain from interfering with the use of those books in the schools' curricula.

The District Court granted summary [immediate] judgment in favor of [the School Board]. In the court's view, "the parties substantially agree[d] about the motivation behind the board's actions," - namely, that

> "the board acted not on religious principles but on its conservative educational philosophy, and on its belief that the nine books removed from the school library and curriculum were irrelevant, vulgar, immoral, and in bad taste, making them educationally unsuitable for the district's junior and senior high school students."

With this factual premise as its background, the court rejected [the students'] contention that their First Amendment rights had been infringed by the Board's actions. Noting that statutes, history, and precedent [prior cases] had vested local school boards with a broad discretion to formulate educational policy, the court concluded that it should not intervene in "'the daily operations of school systems'" unless "'basic constitutional values'" were "'sharply implicate[d]'," and determined that the conditions for such intervention did not exist in the present case. Acknowledging that the "removal [of the books] . . . clearly was content-based," the court nevertheless found no constitutional violation of the requisite magnitude:

> "The board has restricted access only to certain books which the board believed to be, in essence, vulgar. While removal of such books from a school library may . . . reflect a misguided educational philosophy, it does not constitute a sharp and direct infringement of any First Amendment right."

A three-judge panel of the United States Court of Appeals . . . reversed the judgment of the District Court. . . . Judge Newman . . . viewed the case as turning on the contested factual issue of whether petitioners' removal decision was motivated by a justifiable desire to remove books containing vulgarities and sexual explicitness, or rather by an impermissible desire to suppress ideas.

. . . . Our precedents have long recognized certain constitutional limits upon the power of the State to control even the curriculum and classroom. For example, *Meyer v. Nebraska* struck down a state law that forbade the teaching of modern foreign languages in public and private schools, and *Epperson v. Arkansas* declared unconstitutional a state law that prohibited the teaching of the Darwinian theory of evolution in any state-supported school. But the current action does not require us to re-enter this difficult terrain, which *Meyer* and *Epperson* traversed without apparent misgiving. For as this case is presented to us, it does not involve textbooks, or indeed any books that Island Trees students would be required to read. [The students] do not seek in this Court to impose limitations upon their school Board's discretion to prescribe the curricula of the Island Trees schools. On the contrary, the only books at issue in this case are *library* books, books that by their nature are optional rather than required reading. Our adjudication of the present case thus does not intrude into the classroom, or into the compulsory courses taught there. Furthermore, even as to library books, the action before us does not involve the *acquisition* of books. Respondents have not sought to compel their School Board to add to the school library shelves any books that students desire to read. Rather, the only action challenged in this case is the *removal* from school libraries of books originally placed there by the school authorities, or without objection from them.

. . . . [T]he issue before us . . . is a narrow one. . . . [D]oes the First Amendment impose *any* limitations upon the discretion of [the School Board] to remove library books from the Island Trees High School and Junior High School? . . .

The Court has long recognized that local school boards have broad discretion in the management of school affairs. *Epperson* . . . reaffirmed that, by and large, "public education in our Nation is committed to the control of state and local authorities," and that federal courts should not ordinarily "intervene in the resolution of conflicts which arise in the daily operation of school systems." *Tinker v. Des Moines School District* noted that we have "repeatedly emphasized . . . the comprehensive authority of the States and of school officials . . . to prescribe and control conduct in the schools." We have also acknowledged that public schools are vitally important "in the preparation of individuals for participation as citizens," and as vehicles for "inculcating fundamental values necessary to the maintenance of a democratic political system." We are therefore in full agreement with petitioners that local school boards must be permitted "to establish and apply their curriculum in such a way as to transmit community values," and that "there is a legitimate and substantial community interest in promoting respect for authority and traditional values be they social, moral, or political."

At the same time, however, we have necessarily recognized that the discretion of the States and local school boards in matters of education must be exercised in a manner that comports with the transcendent imperatives of the First Amendment. In *West Virginia Board of Education v. Barnette,* we held that under the First Amendment a student in a public school could not be compelled to salute the flag. We reasoned:

> "Boards of Education . . . have, of course, important, delicate, and highly discretionary functions, but none that they may not perform within the limits of the Bill of Rights. That they are educating the young for citizenship is reason for scrupulous protection of Constitutional freedoms of the individual, if we are not to strangle the free mind at its source and teach youth to discount important principles of our government as mere platitudes."

Later cases have consistently followed this rationale. Thus *Epperson* . . . invalidated a State's anti-evolution statute as violative of the Establishment Clause, and reaffirmed the duty of federal courts "to apply the First Amendment's mandate in our educational system where essential to safeguard the fundamental values of freedom of speech and inquiry." And Tinker . . . held that a local school board had infringed the free speech rights of high school and junior high school students by suspending them from school for wearing black armbands in class as a protest against the Government's policy in Vietnam; we stated there that the "comprehensive authority . . . of school officials" must be exercised "consistent with fundamental constitutional safeguards." In sum, students do not "shed their constitutional rights to freedom of speech or expression at the schoolhouse gate," and therefore local school boards must discharge their "important, delicate, and highly discretionary functions" within the limits and constraints of the First Amendment.

The nature of students' First Amendment rights in the context of this case requires further examination. . . . *Barnette* is instructive. There the Court held that students' liberty of conscience could not be infringed in the name of "national unity" or "patriotism." We explained that

> "the action of the local authorities in compelling the flag salute and pledge transcends constitutional limitations on their power and invades the sphere of intellect and spirit which it is the purpose of the First Amendment to our Constitution to reserve from all official control."

Similarly, *Tinker* . . . held that students' rights to freedom of expression of their political views could not be abridged by reliance upon an "undifferentiated fear or apprehension of disturbance" arising from such expression:

> "Any departure from absolute regimentation may cause trouble. Any variation from the majority's opinion may inspire fear. Any word spoken, in class, in the lunchroom, or on the campus, that deviates from the views of another person may start an argument or cause a disturbance. But our Constitution says we must take this risk; and our

history says that it is this sort of hazardous freedom - this kind of openness - that is the basis of
our national strength and of the independence and
vigor of Americans who grow up and live in this
. . . often disputatious society."

In short, "First Amendment rights, applied in light of the
special characteristics of the school environment, are available to . . . students."

Of course, courts should not "intervene in the resolution of
conflicts which arise in the daily operation of school systems" unless "basic constitutional values" are "directly and
sharply implicate[d]" in those conflicts. But we think that
the First Amendment rights of students may be directly and
sharply implicated by the removal of books from the
shelves of a school library. Our precedents have focused
"not only on the role of the First Amendment in fostering
individual self-expression but also on its role in affording
the public access to discussion, debate, and the dissemination of information and ideas." And we have recognized
that "the State may not, consistently with the spirit of the
First Amendment, contract the spectrum of available
knowledge." In keeping with this principle, we have held
that in a variety of contexts "the Constitution protects the
right to receive information and ideas." This right is an inherent corollary of the rights of free speech and press that
are explicitly guaranteed by the Constitution, in two senses.
First, the right to receive ideas follows ineluctably from the
sender's First Amendment right to send them: "The right of
freedom of speech and press . . . embraces the right to dis-
tribute literature, and necessarily protects the right to receive it." "The dissemination of ideas can accomplish
nothing if otherwise willing addressees are not free to receive and consider them. It would be a barren marketplace
of ideas that had only sellers and no buyers."

More importantly, the right to receive ideas is a necessary predicate to the *recipient's* meaningful exercise of his own rights of speech, press, and political freedom. Madison admonished us:

> "A popular Government, without popular information, or the means of acquiring it, is but a Prologue to a Farce or a Tragedy; or, perhaps both. Knowledge will forever govern ignorance: And a people who mean to be their own Governors, must arm themselves with the power which knowledge gives."

As we recognized in *Tinker*, students too are beneficiaries of this principle:

> "In our system, students may not be regarded as closed-circuit recipients of only that which the State chooses to communicate. . . . [S]chool officials cannot suppress 'expressions of feeling with which they do not wish to contend.'"

In sum, just as access to ideas makes it possible for citizens generally to exercise their rights of free speech and press in a meaningful manner, such access prepares students for active and effective participation in the pluralistic, often contentious society in which they will soon be adult members. Of course all First Amendment rights accorded to students must be construed [interpreted] "in light of the special characteristics of the school environment." But the special characteristics of the school *library* make that environment especially appropriate for the recognition of the First Amendment rights of students.

A school library, no less than any other public library, is "a place dedicated to quiet, to knowledge, and to beauty."

Keyishian v. Board of Regents observed that "'students must always remain free to inquire, to study and to evaluate, to gain new maturity and understanding.'" The school library is the principal locus of such freedom. As one District Court has well put it, in the school library

> "a student can literally explore the unknown, and discover areas of interest and thought not covered by the prescribed curriculum. . . . Th[e] student learns that a library is a place to test or expand upon ideas presented to him, in or out of the classroom."

[The School Board] emphasize[s] the inculcative function of secondary education, and argue[s] that [it] must be allowed *unfettered* discretion to "transmit community values" through the Island Trees schools. But that sweeping claim overlooks the unique role of the school library. It appears from the record that use of the Island Trees school libraries is completely voluntary on the part of students. Their selection of books from these libraries is entirely a matter of free choice; the libraries afford them an opportunity at self-education and individual enrichment that is wholly optional. Petitioners might well defend their claim of absolute discretion in matters of *curriculum* by reliance upon their duty to inculcate community values. But we think that petitioners' reliance upon that duty is misplaced where, as here, they attempt to extend their claim of absolute discretion beyond the compulsory environment of the classroom, into the school library and the regime of voluntary inquiry that there holds sway.

In rejecting [the School Board's] claim of absolute discretion to remove books from their school libraries, we do not deny that local school boards have a substantial legitimate role to play in the determination of school library content.

We thus must turn to the question of the extent to which the First Amendment places limitations upon the discretion of [the School Board] to remove books from their libraries. In this inquiry we enjoy the guidance of several precedents. . . . *Barnette* stated:

> "If there is any fixed star in our constitutional constellation, it is that no official, high or petty, can prescribe what shall be orthodox in politics, nationalism, religion, or other matters of opinion. . . . If there are any circumstances which permit an exception, they do not now occur to us."

This doctrine has been reaffirmed in later cases involving education. For example, *Keyishian* . . . noted that "the First Amendment . . . does not tolerate laws that cast a pall of orthodoxy over the classroom." And *Mt. Healthy City Board of Education v. Doyle* recognized First Amendment limitations upon the discretion of a local school board to refuse to re-hire a nontenured teacher. The school board in *Mt. Healthy* had declined to renew respondent Doyle's employment contract, in part because he had exercised his First Amendment rights. Although Doyle did not have tenure, and thus "could have been discharged for no reason whatever," *Mt. Healthy* held that he could "nonetheless establish a claim to reinstatement if the decision not to rehire him was made by reason of his exercise of constitutionally protected First Amendment freedoms." We held further that once Doyle had shown "that his conduct was constitutionally protected, and that this conduct was a 'substantial factor' . . . in the Board's decision not to rehire him," the school board was obliged to show "by a preponderance of the evidence that it would have reached the same decision as to respondent's reemployment even in the absence of the protected conduct."

With respect to the present case, the message of these precedents is clear. [The School Board] rightly possess[es] significant discretion to determine the content of their school libraries. But that discretion may not be exercised in a narrowly partisan or political manner. If a Democratic school board, motivated by party affiliation, ordered the removal of all books written by or in favor of Republicans, few would doubt that the order violated the constitutional rights of the students denied access to those books. The same conclusion would surely apply if an all-white school board, motivated by racial animus, decided to remove all books authored by blacks or advocating racial equality and integration. Our Constitution does not permit the official suppression of *ideas*. Thus whether [the School Board's] removal of books from their school libraries denied [the students] their First Amendment rights depends upon the motivation behind [the School Board's] actions. If [the School Board] *intended* by [its] removal decision to deny [the students] access to ideas with which [the School Board] disagreed, and if this intent was the decisive factor in [the School Board's] decision, then [the School Board has] exercised [its] discretion in violation of the Constitution. To permit such intentions to control official actions would be to encourage the precise sort of officially prescribed orthodoxy unequivocally condemned in *Barnette*. On the other hand, [the students] implicitly concede that an unconstitutional motivation would *not* be demonstrated if it were shown that [the School Board] had decided to remove the books at issue because those books were pervasively vulgar. And again, [the students] concede that if it were demonstrated that the removal decision was based solely upon the "educational suitability" of the books in question, then their removal would be "perfectly permissible." In other words, in [the students'] view such motivations, if decisive of [the School Board's] actions, would not carry the danger of an official suppression of ideas, and thus would not violate [the students'] First Amendment rights.

As noted earlier, nothing in our decision today affects in any way the discretion of a local school board to choose books to *add* to the libraries of their schools. Because we are concerned in this case with the suppression of ideas, our holding today affects only the discretion to *remove* books. In brief, we hold that local school boards may not remove books from school library shelves simply because they dislike the ideas contained in those books and seek by their removal to "prescribe what shall be orthodox in politics, nationalism, religion, or other matters of opinion." Such purposes stand inescapably condemned by our precedents. . . . Affirmed.

Searching Students For Drugs
New Jersey v. T.L.O.

On March 17, 1980, in New Jersey's Piscataway High School, a 14-year-old female freshman (identified as T.L.O.) was brought to the School Office on suspicion of smoking. Assistant Vice Principal Theodore Choplick searched T.L.O.'s purse and found a small amount of marijuana, a substantial amount of money, and papers implicating her in marijuana dealing. Choplick notified the police.

T.L.O. was brought to Police Headquarters where, confronted with the evidence from her purse, she confessed to selling marijuana at Piscataway High. Tried for delinquency in Middlesex County's Juvenile Court, T.L.O. argued that Choplick's search of her purse had been illegal, a violation of her Fourth Amendment right against unreasonable searches and seizures. T.L.O. moved to suppress the evidence, as well as her confession, all of which she alleged were tainted by an unlawful search. The Juvenile Court denied T.L.O.'s motion to suppress, finding that the search was reasonable. T.L.O. was found guilty of delinquency, and on January 8, 1982 sentenced to one year's probation.

T.L.O. appealed the guilty verdict first to the New Jersey Superior Court's Appellate Division, which upheld her conviction, and then to the New Jersey Supreme Court, which reversed her conviction. The reversal, based on the grounds that the search of her purse was unreasonable and thus unconstitutional, was appealed by New Jersey to the United States Supreme Court.

Oral arguments were heard in *New Jersey v. T.L.O* on March 28, 1984 and the 6-3 decision of the Court was announced on January 15, 1985 by Associate Justice Byron White.

The T.L.O. Court

Chief Justice Warren Burger
Appointed Chief Justice by President Nixon
Served 1969 - 1986

Associate Justice William Brennan
Appointed by President Eisenhower
Served 1956 - 1990

Associate Justice Potter Stewart
Appointed by President Eisenhower
Served 1958 - 1981

Associate Justice Byron White
Appointed by President Kennedy
Served 1962 - 1993

Associate Justice Thurgood Marshall
Appointed by President Johnson
Served 1967 - 1991

Associate Justice Harry Blackmun
Appointed by President Nixon
Served 1970 - 1994

Associate Justice Lewis Powell
Appointed by President Nixon
Served 1971 - 1987

Associate Justice William Rehnquist
Appointed by President Nixon
Served 1971 -

Associate Justice John Paul Stevens
Appointed by President Ford
Served 1975 -

The unedited text of *New Jersey v. T.L.O* can be found on page 325, volume 469 of *United States Reports*. Our edited text follows.

NEW JERSEY v. T.L.O.
January 15, 1985

JUSTICE BYRON WHITE: We granted certiorari in [agreed to hear] this case to examine the appropriateness of the exclusionary rule as a remedy for searches carried out in violation of the Fourth Amendment by public school authorities. Our consideration of the proper application of the Fourth Amendment to the public schools, however, has led us to conclude that the search that gave rise to the case now before us did not violate the Fourth Amendment. Accordingly, we here address only the questions of the proper standard for assessing the legality of searches conducted by public school officials and the application of that standard to the facts of this case.

On March 7, 1980, a teacher at Piscataway High School in Middlesex County, N. J., discovered two girls smoking in a lavatory. One of the two girls was the respondent T.L.O., who at that time was a 14-year-old high school freshman. Because smoking in the lavatory was a violation of a school rule, the teacher took the two girls to the Principal's office, where they met with Assistant Vice Principal Theodore Choplick. In response to questioning by Mr. Choplick, T.L.O.'s companion admitted that she had violated the rule. T.L.O., however, denied that she had been smoking in the lavatory and claimed that she did not smoke at all.

Mr. Choplick asked T.L.O. to come into his private office and demanded to see her purse. Opening the purse, he found a pack of cigarettes, which he removed from the purse and held before T.L.O. as he accused her of having lied to him. As he reached into the purse for the cigarettes, Mr. Choplick also noticed a package of cigarette rolling papers. In his experience, possession of rolling papers by high

school students was closely associated with the use of marihuana. Suspecting that a closer examination of the purse
might yield further evidence of drug use, Mr. Choplick proceeded to search the purse thoroughly. The search revealed
a small amount of marihuana, a pipe, a number of empty
plastic bags, a substantial quantity of money in one-dollar
bills, an index card that appeared to be a list of students
who owed T.L.O. money, and two letters that implicated
T.L.O. in marihuana dealing.

Mr. Choplick notified T.L.O.'s mother and the police, and
turned the evidence of drug dealing over to the police. At
the request of the police, T.L.O.'s mother took her daughter to police headquarters, where T.L.O. confessed that she
had been selling marihuana at the high school. On the basis
of the confession and the evidence seized by Mr. Choplick,
the State brought delinquency charges against T.L.O. in the
Juvenile and Domestic Relations Court of Middlesex
County. Contending that Mr. Choplick's search of her
purse violated the Fourth Amendment, T.L.O. moved to
suppress the evidence found in her purse as well as her
confession, which, she argued, was tainted by the allegedly
unlawful search. The Juvenile Court denied the motion to
suppress. Although the court concluded that the Fourth
Amendment did apply to searches carried out by school
officials, it held that

> "a school official may properly conduct a search
> of a student's person if the official has a reason-
> able suspicion that a crime has been or is in the
> process of being committed, or reasonable cause
> to believe that the search is necessary to maintain
> school discipline or enforce school policies."

Applying this standard, the court concluded that the search
conducted by Mr. Choplick was a reasonable one. The ini-

tial decision to open the purse was justified by Mr. Choplick's well-founded suspicion that T.L.O. had violated the rule forbidding smoking in the lavatory. Once the purse was open, evidence of marihuana violations was in plain view, and Mr. Choplick was entitled to conduct a thorough search to determine the nature and extent of T.L.O.'s drug-related activities. Having denied the motion to suppress, the court on March 23, 1981, found T.L.O. to be a delinquent and on January 8, 1982, sentenced her to a year's probation.

On appeal from the final judgment of the Juvenile Court, a divided Appellate Division affirmed [upheld] the trial court's finding that there had been no Fourth Amendment violation, but vacated [annulled] the adjudication of delinquency and remanded [sent back to the lower court] for a determination whether T.L.O. had knowingly and voluntarily waived her Fifth Amendment rights before confessing. T.L.O. appealed the Fourth Amendment ruling, and the Supreme Court of New Jersey reversed the judgment of the Appellate Division and ordered the suppression of the evidence found in T.L.O.'s purse.

The New Jersey Supreme Court agreed with the lower courts that the Fourth Amendment applies to searches conducted by school officials. The court also rejected the State of New Jersey's argument that the exclusionary rule should not be employed to prevent the use in juvenile proceedings of evidence unlawfully seized by school officials. Declining to consider whether applying the rule to the fruits of searches by school officials would have any deterrent value, the court held simply that the precedents of this Court establish that "if an official search violates constitutional rights, the evidence is not admissible in criminal proceedings."

With respect to the question of the legality of the search before it, the court agreed with the Juvenile Court that a warrantless search by a school official does not violate the Fourth Amendment so long as the official "has reasonable grounds to believe that a student possesses evidence of illegal activity or activity that would interfere with school discipline and order." However, the court, with two justices dissenting, sharply disagreed with the Juvenile Court's conclusion that the search of the purse was reasonable. According to the majority, the contents of T.L.O.'s purse had no bearing on the accusation against T.L.O., for possession of cigarettes (as opposed to smoking them in the lavatory) did not violate school rules, and a mere desire for evidence that would impeach T.L.O.'s claim that she did not smoke cigarettes could not justify the search. Moreover, even if a reasonable suspicion that T.L.O. had cigarettes in her purse would justify a search, Mr. Choplick had no such suspicion, as no one had furnished him with any specific information that there were cigarettes in the purse. Finally, leaving aside the question whether Mr. Choplick was justified in opening the purse, the court held that the evidence of drug use that he saw inside did not justify the extensive "rummaging" through T.L.O.'s papers and effects that followed.

We granted the State of New Jersey's petition for certiorari. Although the State had argued in the Supreme Court of New Jersey that the search of T.L.O.'s purse did not violate the Fourth Amendment, the petition for certiorari raised only the question whether the exclusionary rule should operate to bar consideration in juvenile delinquency proceedings of evidence unlawfully seized by a school official without the involvement of law enforcement officers. When this case was first argued last Term, the State conceded for the purpose of argument that the standard devised by the New Jersey Supreme Court for determining the legality of school searches was appropriate and that the court had correctly applied that standard; the State contended only that the remedial purposes of the exclusionary rule were not well served by applying it to searches conducted by public authorities not primarily engaged in law enforcement.

Although we originally granted certiorari to decide the issue of the appropriate remedy in juvenile court proceedings for unlawful school searches, our doubts regarding the wisdom of deciding that question in isolation from the broader question of what limits, if any, the Fourth Amendment places on the activities of school authorities prompted us to order reargument on that question. Having heard argument on the legality of the search of T.L.O.'s purse, we are satisfied that the search did not violate the Fourth Amendment.

In determining whether the search at issue in this case violated the Fourth Amendment, we are faced initially with the question whether that Amendment's prohibition on unreasonable searches and seizures applies to searches conducted by public school officials. We hold that it does.

It is now beyond dispute that "the Federal Constitution, by virtue of the Fourteenth Amendment, prohibits unreasonable searches and seizures by state officers." Equally indisputable is the proposition that the Fourteenth Amendment protects the rights of students against encroachment by public school officials:

> "The Fourteenth Amendment, as now applied to the States, protects the citizen against the State itself and all of its creatures - Boards of Education not excepted. These have, of course, important, delicate, and highly discretionary functions, but none that they may not perform within the limits of the Bill of Rights. That they are educating the young for citizenship is reason for scrupulous

protection of Constitutional freedoms of the individual, if we are not to strangle the free mind at its source and teach youth to discount important principles of our government as mere platitudes."

These two propositions - that the Fourth Amendment applies to the States through the Fourteenth Amendment, and that the actions of public school officials are subject to the limits placed on state action by the Fourteenth Amendment - might appear sufficient to answer the suggestion that the Fourth Amendment does not proscribe unreasonable searches by school officials. On reargument, however, the State of New Jersey has argued that the history of the Fourth Amendment indicates that the Amendment was intended to regulate only searches and seizures carried out by law enforcement officers; accordingly, although public school officials are concededly state agents for purposes of the Fourteenth Amendment, the Fourth Amendment creates no rights enforceable against them.

It may well be true that the evil toward which the Fourth Amendment was primarily directed was the resurrection of the pre-Revolutionary practice of using general warrants or "writs of assistance" to authorize searches for contraband by officers of the Crown. But this Court has never limited the Amendment's prohibition on unreasonable searches and seizures to operations conducted by the police. Rather, the Court has long spoken of the Fourth Amendment's strictures as restraints imposed upon "governmental action" - that is, "upon the activities of sovereign authority." Accordingly, we have held the Fourth Amendment applicable to the activities of civil as well as criminal authorities: building inspectors, Occupational Safety and Health Act inspectors, and even firemen entering privately owned premises to battle a fire, are all subject to the restraints imposed by the Fourth Amendment. As we observed in *Ca-*

mara v. Municipal Court, "[t]he basic purpose of this Amendment, as recognized in countless decisions of this Court, is to safeguard the privacy and security of individuals against arbitrary invasions by governmental officials." Because the individual's interest in privacy and personal security "suffers whether the government's motivation is to investigate violations of criminal laws or breaches of other statutory or regulatory standards," it would be "anomalous to say that the individual and his private property are fully protected by the Fourth Amendment only when the individual is suspected of criminal behavior."

Notwithstanding the general applicability of the Fourth Amendment to the activities of civil authorities, a few courts have concluded that school officials are exempt from the dictates of the Fourth Amendment by virtue of the special nature of their authority over schoolchildren. Teachers and school administrators, it is said, act *in loco parentis* [in place of the parent] in their dealings with students: their authority is that of the parent, not the State, and is therefore not subject to the limits of the Fourth Amendment.

Such reasoning is in tension with contemporary reality and the teachings of this Court. We have held school officials subject to the commands of the First Amendment, and the Due Process Clause of the Fourteenth Amendment. If school authorities are state actors for purposes of the constitutional guarantees of freedom of expression and due process, it is difficult to understand why they should be deemed to be exercising parental rather than public authority when conducting searches of their students. More generally, the Court has recognized that "the concept of parental delegation" as a source of school authority is not entirely "consonant with compulsory education laws." Today's public school officials do not merely exercise authority voluntarily conferred on them by individual parents; rather, they act in furtherance of publicly mandated educational and disciplinary policies. In carrying out searches and other disciplinary functions pursuant to such policies, school officials act as representatives of the State, not merely as surrogates for the parents, and they cannot claim the parents' immunity from the strictures of the Fourth Amendment.

To hold that the Fourth Amendment applies to searches conducted by school authorities is only to begin the inquiry into the standards governing such searches. Although the underlying command of the Fourth Amendment is always that searches and seizures be reasonable, what is reasonable depends on the context within which a search takes place. The determination of the standard of reasonableness governing any specific class of searches requires "balancing the need to search against the invasion which the search entails." On one side of the balance are arrayed the individual's legitimate expectations of privacy and personal security; on the other, the government's need for effective methods to deal with breaches of public order.

We have recognized that even a limited search of the person is a substantial invasion of privacy. We have also recognized that searches of closed items of personal luggage are intrusions on protected privacy interests, for "the Fourth Amendment provides protection to the owner of every container that conceals its contents from plain view." A search of a child's person or of a closed purse or other bag carried on her person, no less than a similar search carried out on an adult, is undoubtedly a severe violation of subjective expectations of privacy.

Of course, the Fourth Amendment does not protect subjective expectations of privacy that are unreasonable or otherwise "illegitimate." To receive the protection of the

Fourth Amendment, an expectation of privacy must be one that society is "prepared to recognize as legitimate." The State of New Jersey has argued that because of the pervasive supervision to which children in the schools are necessarily subject, a child has virtually no legitimate expectation of privacy in articles of personal property "unnecessarily" carried into a school. This argument has two factual premises: (1) the fundamental incompatibility of expectations of privacy with the maintenance of a sound educational environment; and (2) the minimal interest of the child in bringing any items of personal property into the school. Both premises are severely flawed.

Although this Court may take notice of the difficulty of maintaining discipline in the public schools today, the situation is not so dire that students in the schools may claim no legitimate expectations of privacy. We have recently recognized that the need to maintain order in a prison is such that prisoners retain no legitimate expectations of privacy in their cells, but it goes almost without saying that "[t]he prisoner and the schoolchild stand in wholly different circumstances, separated by the harsh facts of criminal conviction and incarceration." We are not yet ready to hold that the schools and the prisons need be equated for purposes of the Fourth Amendment.

Nor does the State's suggestion that children have no legitimate need to bring personal property into the schools seem well anchored in reality. Students at a minimum must bring to school not only the supplies needed for their studies, but also keys, money, and the necessaries of personal hygiene and grooming. In addition, students may carry on their persons or in purses or wallets such nondisruptive yet highly personal items as photographs, letters, and diaries. Finally, students may have perfectly legitimate reasons to carry with them articles of property needed in connection with extracurricular or recreational activities. In short, schoolchildren may find it necessary to carry with them a variety of legitimate, noncontraband items, and there is no reason to conclude that they have necessarily waived all rights to privacy in such items merely by bringing them onto school grounds.

Against the child's interest in privacy must be set the substantial interest of teachers and administrators in maintaining discipline in the classroom and on school grounds. Maintaining order in the classroom has never been easy, but in recent years, school disorder has often taken particularly ugly forms: drug use and violent crime in the schools have become major social problems. Even in schools that have been spared the most severe disciplinary problems, the preservation of order and a proper educational environment requires close supervision of schoolchildren, as well as the enforcement of rules against conduct that would be perfectly permissible if undertaken by an adult. "Events calling for discipline are frequent occurrences and sometimes require immediate, effective action." Accordingly, we have recognized that maintaining security and order in the schools requires a certain degree of flexibility in school disciplinary procedures, and we have respected the value of preserving the informality of the student-teacher relationship.

How, then, should we strike the balance between the schoolchild's legitimate expectations of privacy and the school's equally legitimate need to maintain an environment in which learning can take place? It is evident that the school setting requires some easing of the restrictions to which searches by public authorities are ordinarily subject. The warrant requirement, in particular, is unsuited to the school environment: requiring a teacher to obtain a warrant before searching a child suspected of an infraction of school rules (or of the criminal law) would unduly interfere with the maintenance of the swift and informal disciplinary procedures needed in the schools. Just as we have in other cases dispensed with the warrant requirement when "the burden of obtaining a warrant is likely to frustrate the governmental purpose behind the search," we hold today that school officials need not obtain a warrant before searching a student who is under their authority.

The school setting also requires some modification of the level of suspicion of illicit activity needed to justify a search. Ordinarily, a search - even one that may permissibly be carried out without a warrant - must be based upon "probable cause" to believe that a violation of the law has occurred. However, "probable cause" is not an irreducible requirement of a valid search. The fundamental command of the Fourth Amendment is that searches and seizures be reasonable, and although "both the concept of probable cause and the requirement of a warrant bear on the reasonableness of a search, . . . in certain limited circumstances neither is required." Thus, we have in a number of cases recognized the legality of searches and seizures based on suspicions that, although "reasonable," do not rise to the level of probable cause. Where a careful balancing of governmental and private interests suggests that the public interest is best served by a Fourth Amendment standard of reasonableness that stops short of probable cause, we have not hesitated to adopt such a standard.

We join the majority of courts that have examined this issue in concluding that the accommodation of the privacy interests of schoolchildren with the substantial need of teachers and administrators for freedom to maintain order in the schools does not require strict adherence to the requirement that searches be based on probable cause to believe that the subject of the search has violated or is violating the law. Rather, the legality of a search of a student should depend simply on the reasonableness, under all the circumstances, of the search. Determining the reasonableness of any search involves a twofold inquiry: first, one must consider "whether the . . . action was justified at its inception"; second, one must determine whether the search as actually conducted "was reasonably related in scope to the circumstances which justified the interference in the first place." Under ordinary circumstances, a search of a student by a teacher or other school official will be "justified at its inception" when there are reasonable grounds for suspecting that the search will turn up evidence that the student has violated or is violating either the law or the rules of the school. Such a search will be permissible in its scope when the measures adopted are reasonably related to the objectives of the search and not excessively intrusive in light of the age and sex of the student and the nature of the infraction.

This standard will, we trust, neither unduly burden the efforts of school authorities to maintain order in their schools nor authorize unrestrained intrusions upon the privacy of schoolchildren. By focusing attention on the question of reasonableness, the standard will spare teachers and school administrators the necessity of schooling themselves in the niceties of probable cause and permit them to regulate their conduct according to the dictates of reason and common sense. At the same time, the reasonableness standard should ensure that the interests of students will be invaded no more than is necessary to achieve the legitimate end of preserving order in the schools.

There remains the question of the legality of the search in this case. We recognize that the "reasonable grounds" standard applied by the New Jersey Supreme Court in its consideration of this question is not substantially different from the standard that we have adopted today. Nonetheless, we believe that the New Jersey court's application of that standard to strike down the search of T.L.O.'s purse reflects a somewhat crabbed notion of reasonableness. Our review of the facts surrounding the search leads us to conclude that the search was in no sense unreasonable for Fourth Amendment purposes.

The incident that gave rise to this case actually involved two separate searches, with the first - the search for cigarettes - providing the suspicion that gave rise to the second - the search for marihuana. Although it is the fruits of the second search that are at issue here, the validity of the search for marihuana must depend on the reasonableness of the initial search for cigarettes, as there would have been no reason to suspect that T.L.O. possessed marihuana had the first search not taken place. Accordingly, it is to the search for cigarettes that we first turn our attention.

The New Jersey Supreme Court pointed to two grounds for its holding that the search for cigarettes was unreasonable. First, the court observed that possession of cigarettes was not in itself illegal or a violation of school rules. Because the contents of T.L.O.'s purse would therefore have "no direct bearing on the infraction" of which she was accused (smoking in a lavatory where smoking was prohibited), there was no reason to search her purse. Second, even assuming that a search of T.L.O.'s purse might under some circumstances be reasonable in light of the accusation made against T.L.O., the New Jersey court concluded that Mr. Choplick in this particular case had no reasonable grounds to suspect that T.L.O. had cigarettes in her purse. At best, according to the court, Mr. Choplick had "a good hunch."

Both these conclusions are implausible. T.L.O. had been accused of smoking, and had denied the accusation in the strongest possible terms when she stated that she did not smoke at all. Surely it cannot be said that under these circumstances, T.L.O.'s possession of cigarettes would be irrelevant to the charges against her or to her response to those charges. T.L.O.'s possession of cigarettes, once it was discovered, would both corroborate the report that she had been smoking and undermine the credibility of her defense to the charge of smoking. To be sure, the discovery of the cigarettes would not prove that T.L.O. had been smoking in the lavatory; nor would it, strictly speaking, necessarily be inconsistent with her claim that she did not smoke at all. But it is universally recognized that evidence, to be relevant to an inquiry, need not conclusively prove the ultimate fact in issue, but only have "any tendency to make the existence of any fact that is of consequence to the determination of the action more probable or less probable than it would be without the evidence." The relevance of T.L.O.'s possession of cigarettes to the question whether she had been smoking and to the credibility of her denial that she smoked supplied the necessary "nexus" between the item searched for and the infraction under investigation. Thus, if Mr. Choplick in fact had a reasonable suspicion that T.L.O. had cigarettes in her purse, the search was justified despite the fact that the cigarettes, if found, would constitute "mere evidence" of a violation.

Of course, the New Jersey Supreme Court also held that Mr. Choplick had no reasonable suspicion that the purse would contain cigarettes. This conclusion is puzzling. A teacher had reported that T.L.O. was smoking in the lavatory. Certainly this report gave Mr. Choplick reason to suspect that T.L.O. was carrying cigarettes with her; and if she did have cigarettes, her purse was the obvious place in which to find them. Mr. Choplick's suspicion that there were cigarettes in the purse was not an "inchoate and unparticularized suspicion or 'hunch'"; rather, it was the sort of "common-sense conclusio[n] about human behavior" upon which "practical people" - including government officials - are entitled to rely. Of course, even if the teacher's report were true, T.L.O. *might* not have had a pack of cigarettes with her; she might have borrowed a cigarette from someone else or have been sharing a cigarette with another student. But the requirement of reasonable suspicion is not a requirement of absolute certainty: "sufficient probability, not certainty, is the touchstone of reasonableness under the Fourth Amendment. . . ." Because the hypothesis that T.L.O. was carrying cigarettes in her purse was itself not unreasonable, it is irrelevant that other hypotheses were also consistent with the teacher's accusation. Accordingly, it cannot be said that Mr. Choplick acted unreasonably when he examined T.L.O.'s purse to see if it contained cigarettes.

Our conclusion that Mr. Choplick's decision to open T.L.O.'s purse was reasonable brings us to the question of the further search for marihuana once the pack of cigarettes was located. The suspicion upon which the search for marihuana was founded was provided when Mr. Choplick observed a package of rolling papers in the purse as he removed the pack of cigarettes. Although T.L.O. does not dispute the reasonableness of Mr. Choplick's belief that the rolling papers indicated the presence of marihuana, she does contend that the scope of the search Mr. Choplick conducted exceeded permissible bounds when he seized and read certain letters that implicated T.L.O. in drug dealing. This argument, too, is unpersuasive. The discovery of the rolling papers concededly gave rise to a reasonable suspicion that T.L.O. was carrying marihuana as well as cigarettes in her purse. This suspicion justified further exploration of T.L.O.'s purse, which turned up more evidence of drug-related activities: a pipe, a number of plastic bags of the type commonly used to store marihuana, a small quantity of marihuana, and a fairly substantial amount of money.

Under these circumstances, it was not unreasonable to extend the search to a separate zippered compartment of the purse; and when a search of that compartment revealed an index card containing a list of "people who owe me money" as well as two letters, the inference that T.L.O. was involved in marihuana trafficking was substantial enough to justify Mr. Choplick in examining the letters to determine whether they contained any further evidence. In short, we cannot conclude that the search for marihuana was unreasonable in any respect.

Because the search resulting in the discovery of the evidence of marihuana dealing by T.L.O. was reasonable, the New Jersey Supreme Court's decision to exclude that evidence from T.L.O.'s juvenile delinquency proceedings on Fourth Amendment grounds was erroneous. Accordingly, the judgment of the Supreme Court of New Jersey is reversed.

"Equal Time" For Creation Science
Edwards v. Aguillard

Charles Darwin's *Origin of Species*, postulating the theory of evolution, was first published in 1858. One hundred twenty-three years later, the State of Louisiana demanded "equal time" for creation science. In 1981 the Louisiana State Legislature passed the Creationism Act, known officially as "The Act for Balanced Treatment for Creation-Science and Evolution-Science in Public Schools Instruction." This law forbade teaching the theory of evolution, called evolution-science, in the public schools, unless equal time was given to the teaching of creation-science. Based on a literal interpretation of the Book of Genesis, creation science holds that mankind was instantaneously created by a supernatural being.

Don Aguillard headed a group of public school teachers, parents, and religious leaders who challenged the constitutionality of the Creationism Act. They alleged that creation science was a religious doctrine and that restructuring the science curriculum of the public schools to teach it was violation of the First Amendment's Establishment Clause. Louisiana officials, including Governor Edwin Edwards, defended the Creationism Act as a protection of academic freedom. The United States District Court ruled that the Creationism Act violated the Establishment Clause. Louisiana appealed to the United States Court of Appeals. The Court of Appeals affirmed the District Court's judgment. Louisiana appealed to the United States Supreme Court.

Oral arguments were heard in *Edwards v. Aguillard* on December 10, 1986 and the 7-2 decision of the United States Supreme Court was announced on June 19, 1987 by Associate Justice William Brennan.

The Edwards Court

Chief Justice William Rehnquist
Appointed Chief Justice by President Reagan
Appointed Associate Justice by President Nixon
Served 1971 -

Associate Justice William Brennan
Appointed by President Eisenhower
Served 1956 - 1990

Associate Justice Byron White
Appointed by President Kennedy
Served 1962 - 1993

Associate Justice Thurgood Marshall
Appointed by President Johnson
Served 1967 - 1991

Associate Justice Harry Blackmun
Appointed by President Nixon
Served 1970 - 1994

Associate Justice John Paul Stevens
Appointed by President Ford
Served 1975 -

Associate Justice Sandra Day O'Connor
Appointed by President Reagan
Served 1981 -

Associate Justice Antonin Scalia
Appointed by President Reagan
Served 1986 -

Associate Justice Anthony Kennedy
Appointed by President Reagan
Served 1988 -

The unedited text of *Edwards v. Aguillard* can be found on page 578, volume 482 of *United States Reports*. Our edited text follows.

EDWARDS v. AGUILLARD
June 19, 1987

JUSTICE WILLIAM BRENNAN: The question for decision is whether Louisiana's "Balanced Treatment for Creation-Science and Evolution-Science in Public School Instruction" Act (Creationism Act) is . . . violative of the Establishment Clause of the First Amendment.

The Creationism Act forbids the teaching of the theory of evolution in public schools unless accompanied by instruction in "creation science." No school is required to teach evolution or creation science. If either is taught, however, the other must also be taught. The theories of evolution and creation science are statutorily defined as "the scientific evidences for [creation or evolution] and inferences from those scientific evidences."

Appellees, who include parents of children attending Louisiana public schools, Louisiana teachers, and religious leaders, challenged the constitutionality of the Act in District Court, seeking an injunction [court order stopping an action]. . . . Appellants, Louisiana officials charged with implementing the Act, defended on the ground that the purpose of the Act is to protect a legitimate secular interest, namely, academic freedom. Appellees attacked the Act as . . . violat[ive of] the Establishment Clause. . . . The District Court granted the[ir] motion. The court held that there can be no valid secular reason for prohibiting the teaching of evolution, a theory historically opposed by some religious denominations. The court further concluded that "the teaching of 'creation-science' and 'creationism,' as contemplated by the statute, involves teaching 'tailored to the principles' of a particular religious sect or group of sects." The District Court therefore held that the Creationism Act violated the Establishment Clause either because it prohibited the teaching of evolution or because it required the teaching of creation science with the purpose of advancing a particular religious doctrine.

The Court of Appeals affirmed [upheld]. The court observed that the statute's avowed purpose of protecting academic freedom was inconsistent with requiring, upon risk of sanction, the teaching of creation science whenever evolution is taught. The court found that the Louisiana Legislature's actual intent was "to discredit evolution by counterbalancing its teaching at every turn with the teaching of creationism, a religious belief." Because the Creationism Act was thus a law furthering a particular religious belief, the Court of Appeals held that the Act violated the Establishment Clause. A suggestion for rehearing en banc [with the entire court participating in the decision] was denied over a dissent. We noted probable jurisdiction [authority] and now affirm.

The Establishment Clause forbids the enactment of any law "respecting an establishment of religion." The Court has applied a three-pronged test to determine whether legislation comports with the Establishment Clause. First, the legislature must have adopted the law with a secular purpose. Second, the statute's principal or primary effect must be one that neither advances nor inhibits religion. Third, the statute must not result in an excessive entanglement of government with religion. State action violates the Establishment Clause if it fails to satisfy any of these prongs.

In this case, the Court must determine whether the Establishment Clause was violated in the special context of the public elementary and secondary school system. States and local school boards are generally afforded considerable discretion in operating public schools. "At the same time . . .

we have necessarily recognized that the discretion of the States and local school boards in matters of education must be exercised in a manner that comports with the transcendent imperatives of the First Amendment."

The Court has been particularly vigilant in monitoring compliance with the Establishment Clause in elementary and secondary schools. Families entrust public schools with the education of their children, but condition their trust on the understanding that the classroom will not purposely be used to advance religious views that may conflict with the private beliefs of the student and his or her family. Students in such institutions are impressionable and their attendance is involuntary. The State exerts great authority and coercive power through mandatory attendance requirements, and because of the students' emulation of teachers as role models and the children's susceptibility to peer pressure. Furthermore, "[t]he public school is at once the symbol of our democracy and the most pervasive means for promoting our common destiny. In no activity of the State is it more vital to keep out divisive forces than in its schools. . . ."

Consequently, the Court has been required often to invalidate statutes which advance religion in public elementary and secondary schools.

Therefore, in employing the three-pronged *Lemon [v. Kurtzman]* test, we must do so mindful of the particular concerns that arise in the context of public elementary and secondary schools. We now turn to the evaluation of the Act under the *Lemon* test.

Lemon's first prong focuses on the purpose that animated adoption of the Act. "The purpose prong of the *Lemon* test asks whether government's actual purpose is to endorse or disapprove of religion." A governmental intention to promote religion is clear when the State enacts a law to serve a religious purpose. This intention may be evidenced by promotion of religion in general, or by advancement of a particular religious belief. If the law was enacted for the purpose of endorsing religion, "no consideration of the second or third criteria [of *Lemon*] is necessary." In this case, appellants have identified no clear secular purpose for the Louisiana Act.

True, the Act's stated purpose is to protect academic freedom. This phrase might, in common parlance, be understood as referring to enhancing the freedom of teachers to teach what they will. The Court of Appeals, however, correctly concluded that the Act was not designed to further that goal. We find no merit in the State's argument that the "legislature may not [have] use[d] the terms 'academic freedom' in the correct legal sense. They might have [had] in mind, instead, a basic concept of fairness; teaching all of the evidence." Even if "academic freedom" is read to mean "teaching all of the evidence" with respect to the origin of human beings, the Act does not further this purpose. The goal of providing a more comprehensive science curriculum is not furthered either by outlawing the teaching of evolution or by requiring the teaching of creation science.

While the Court is normally deferential to a State's articulation of a secular purpose, it is required that the statement of such purpose be sincere and not a sham. As Justice O'Connor stated in *Wallace [v. Jaffree]*: "It is not a trivial matter, however, to require that the legislature manifest a secular purpose and omit all sectarian endorsements from its laws. That requirement is precisely tailored to the Establishment Clause's purpose of assuring that Government not intentionally endorse religion or a religious practice."

It is clear from the legislative history that the purpose of the legislative sponsor, Senator Bill Keith, was to narrow the science curriculum. During the legislative hearings, Senator Keith stated: "My preference would be that neither [creationism nor evolution] be taught." Such a ban on teaching does not promote - indeed, it undermines - the provision of a comprehensive scientific education.

It is equally clear that requiring schools to teach creation science with evolution does not advance academic freedom. The Act does not grant teachers a flexibility that they did not already possess to supplant the present science curriculum with the presentation of theories, besides evolution, about the origin of life. Indeed, the Court of Appeals found that no law prohibited Louisiana public school teachers from teaching any scientific theory. As the president of the Louisiana Science Teachers Association testified, "[a]ny scientific concept that's based on established fact can be included in our curriculum already, and no legislation allowing this is necessary." The Act provides Louisiana schoolteachers with no new authority. Thus the stated purpose is not furthered by it.

The Alabama statute held unconstitutional in *Wallace v. Jaffree*, is analogous. In *Wallace*, the State characterized its new law as one designed to provide a 1-minute period for meditation. We rejected that stated purpose as insufficient, because a previously adopted Alabama law already provided for such a 1-minute period. Thus, in this case, as in *Wallace*, "[a]ppellants have not identified any secular purpose that was not fully served by [existing state law] before the enactment of [the statute in question]."

Furthermore, the goal of basic "fairness" is hardly furthered by the Act's discriminatory preference for the teaching of creation science and against the teaching of evolution.

While requiring that curriculum guides be developed for creation science, the Act says nothing of comparable guides for evolution. Similarly, resource services are supplied for creation science but not for evolution. Only "creation scientists" can serve on the panel that supplies the resource services. The Act forbids school boards to discriminate against anyone who "chooses to be a creation-scientist" or to teach "creationism," but fails to protect those who choose to teach evolution or any other non-creation science theory, or who refuse to teach creation science.

If the Louisiana Legislature's purpose was solely to maximize the comprehensiveness and effectiveness of science instruction, it would have encouraged the teaching of all scientific theories about the origins of humankind. But under the Act's requirements, teachers who were once free to teach any and all facets of this subject are now unable to do so. Moreover, the Act fails even to ensure that creation science will be taught, but instead requires the teaching of this theory only when the theory of evolution is taught. Thus we agree with the Court of Appeals' conclusion that the Act does not serve to protect academic freedom, but has the distinctly different purpose of discrediting "evolution by counterbalancing its teaching at every turn with the teaching of creationism. . . ."

Stone v. Graham invalidated the State's requirement that the Ten Commandments be posted in public classrooms. "The Ten Commandments are undeniably a sacred text in the Jewish and Christian faiths, and no legislative recitation of a supposed secular purpose can blind us to that fact." As a result, the contention that the law was designed to provide instruction on a "fundamental legal code" was "not sufficient to avoid conflict with the First Amendment." Similarly *Abington School District v. Schempp* held unconstitutional a statute "requiring the selection and reading at the opening of the school day of verses from the Holy Bible and the recitation of the Lord's Prayer by the students in unison," despite the proffer of such secular purposes as the "promotion of moral values, the contradiction to the materialistic trends of our times, the perpetuation of our institutions and the teaching of literature."

As in *Stone* and *Abington*, we need not be blind in this case to the legislature's preeminent religious purpose in enacting this statute. There is a historic and contemporaneous link between the teachings of certain religious denominations and the teaching of evolution. It was this link that concerned the Court in *Epperson v. Arkansas*, which also involved a . . . challenge to a statute regulating the teaching of evolution. In that case, the Court reviewed an Arkansas statute that made it unlawful for an instructor to teach evolution or to use a textbook that referred to this scientific theory. Although the Arkansas antievolution law did not explicitly state its predominate religious purpose, the Court could not ignore that "[t]he statute was a product of the upsurge of 'fundamentalist' religious fervor" that has long viewed this particular scientific theory as contradicting the literal interpretation of the Bible. After reviewing the history of antievolution statutes, the Court determined that "there can be no doubt that the motivation for the [Arkansas] law was the same [as other antievolution statutes]: to suppress the teaching of a theory which, it was thought, 'denied' the divine creation of man." The Court found that there can be no legitimate state interest in protecting particular religions from scientific views "distasteful to them," and concluded "that the First Amendment does not permit the State to require that teaching and learning must be tailored to the principles or prohibitions of any religious sect or dogma."

These same historic and contemporaneous antagonisms between the teachings of certain religious denominations and the teaching of evolution are present in this case. The preeminent purpose of the Louisiana Legislature was clearly to advance the religious viewpoint that a supernatural being created humankind. The term "creation science" was defined as embracing this particular religious doctrine by those responsible for the passage of the Creationism Act. Senator Keith's leading expert on creation science, Edward Boudreaux, testified at the legislative hearings that the theory of creation science included belief in the existence of a supernatural creator. Senator Keith also cited testimony from other experts to support the creation-science view that "a creator [was] responsible for the universe and everything in it." The legislative history therefore reveals that the term "creation science," as contemplated by the legislature that adopted this Act, embodies the religious belief that a supernatural creator was responsible for the creation of humankind.

Furthermore, it is not happenstance that the legislature required the teaching of a theory that coincided with this religious view. The legislative history documents that the Act's primary purpose was to change the science curriculum of public schools in order to provide persuasive advantage to a particular religious doctrine that rejects the factual basis of evolution in its entirety. The sponsor of the Creationism Act, Senator Keith, explained during the legislative hearings that his disdain for the theory of evolution resulted from the support that evolution supplied to views contrary to his own religious beliefs. According to Senator Keith, the theory of evolution was consonant with the "cardinal principle[s] of religious humanism, secular humanism, theological liberalism, aetheistism [sic]." The state senator repeatedly stated that scientific evidence supporting his religious views should be included in the public school curriculum to redress the fact that the theory of evolution incidentally coincided with what he characterized as religious beliefs antithetical to his own. The legislation therefore sought to alter the science curriculum to reflect endorsement of a religious view that is antagonistic to the theory of evolution.

In this case, the purpose of the Creationism Act was to restructure the science curriculum to conform with a particular religious viewpoint. Out of many possible science subjects taught in the public schools, the legislature chose to affect the teaching of the one scientific theory that historically has been opposed by certain religious sects. As in *Epperson*, the legislature passed the Act to give preference to those religious groups which have as one of their tenets the creation of humankind by a divine creator. The "overriding fact" that confronted the Court in *Epperson* was "that Arkansas' law selects from the body of knowledge a particular segment which it proscribes for the sole reason that it is deemed to conflict with . . . a particular interpretation of the Book of Genesis by a particular religious group." Similarly, the Creationism Act is designed *either* to promote the theory of creation science which embodies a particular religious tenet by requiring that creation science be taught whenever evolution is taught *or* to prohibit the teaching of a scientific theory disfavored by certain religious sects by forbidding the teaching of evolution when creation science is not also taught. The Establishment Clause, however, "forbids *alike* the preference of a religious doctrine *or* the prohibition of theory which is deemed antagonistic to a particular dogma." Because the primary purpose of the Creationism Act is to advance a particular religious belief, the Act endorses religion in violation of the First Amendment.

We do not imply that a legislature could never require that scientific critiques of prevailing scientific theories be taught.

Indeed, the Court acknowledged in *Stone* that its decision forbidding the posting of the Ten Commandments did not mean that no use could ever be made of the Ten Commandments, or that the Ten Commandments played an exclusively religious role in the history of Western Civilization. In a similar way, teaching a variety of scientific theories about the origins of humankind to schoolchildren might be validly done with the clear secular intent of enhancing the effectiveness of science instruction. But because the primary purpose of the Creationism Act is to endorse a particular religious doctrine, the Act furthers religion in violation of the Establishment Clause.

Appellants contend that genuine issues of material fact remain in dispute. . . . A court's finding of improper purpose behind a statute is appropriately determined by the statute on its face, its legislative history, or its interpretation by a responsible administrative agency. The plain meaning of the statute's words, enlightened by their context and the contemporaneous legislative history, can control the determination of legislative purpose. Moreover, in determining the legislative purpose of a statute, the Court has also considered the historical context of the statute. . . and the specific sequence of events leading to passage of the statute. . . .

The District Court, in its discretion, properly concluded that a Monday-morning "battle of the experts" over possible technical meanings of terms in the statute would not illuminate the contemporaneous purpose of the Louisiana Legislature when it made the law. We therefore conclude that the District Court did not err. . . .

The Louisiana Creationism Act advances a religious doctrine by requiring either the banishment of the theory of evolution from public school classrooms or the presentation of a religious viewpoint that rejects evolution in its entirety. The Act violates the Establishment Clause of the First Amendment because it seeks to employ the symbolic and financial support of government to achieve a religious purpose. The judgment of the Court of Appeals therefore is affirmed.

Censoring Student Newspapers
Hazelwood Schools v. Kuhlmeier

Spectrum was the student newspaper of Hazelwood, Missouri's East High School. Written and edited by students in the school's journalism class, *Spectrum* was funded by the School District, supervised by a journalism teacher, and always reviewed, prior to publication, by the principal.

Principal Robert Eugene Reynolds, after being shown page proofs of the proposed May 13, 1983 issue of *Spectrum,* ordered two pages cut in order to delete two articles he found objectionable. The Principal ordered deleted an "all names have been changed" article dealing with three pregnant students, which he believed did not adequately protect the girls' anonymity, and an article on the impact of divorce, in which a named student made comments about a parent, which Reynolds felt were unfair.

Claiming that the deletion of the articles on pregnancy and divorce were a violation of their First Amendment rights, student staff members of *Spectrum,* including Cathy Kuhlmeier, sued their principal, journalism teacher, and the Hazelwood School District in the United States District Court. On May 9, 1985 the District Court ruled for the School District, finding that no violation of the students' First Amendment rights had occurred. The students appealed to the United States Court of Appeals. On July 7, 1986 the Court of Appeals, reversing the decision of the District Court, ruled that a violation of the students' First Amendment rights had occurred. The Hazelwood School District appealed to the United States Supreme Court.

Oral arguments were heard in *Hazelwood Schools v. Kuhlmeier* on October 13, 1987 and the decision of the Court was announced on January 13, 1988 by Associate Justice Byron White.

The Hazelwood Court

Chief Justice William Rehnquist
Appointed Chief Justice by President Reagan
Appointed Associate Justice by President Nixon
Served 1971 -

Associate Justice William Brennan
Appointed by President Eisenhower
Served 1956 - 1990

Associate Justice Byron White
Appointed by President Kennedy
Served 1962 - 1993

Associate Justice Thurgood Marshall
Appointed by President Johnson
Served 1967 - 1991

Associate Justice Harry Blackmun
Appointed by President Nixon
Served 1970 - 1994

Associate Justice John Paul Stevens
Appointed by President Ford
Served 1975 -

Associate Justice Sandra Day O'Connor
Appointed by President Reagan
Served 1981 -

Associate Justice Antonin Scalia
Appointed by President Reagan
Served 1986 -

Associate Justice Anthony Kennedy
Appointed by President Reagan
Served 1988 -

The unedited text of *Hazelwood Schools v. Kuhlmeier* can be found on page 260, volume 484 of *United States Reports*. Our edited text follows.

HAZELWOOD SCHOOLS
v. KUHLMEIER
January 13, 1988

JUSTICE BYRON WHITE: This case concerns the extent to which educators may exercise editorial control over the contents of a high school newspaper produced as part of the school's journalism curriculum.

Petitioners are the Hazelwood School District in St. Louis County, Missouri; various school officials; Robert Eugene Reynolds, the principal of Hazelwood East High School; and Howard Emerson, a teacher in the school district. Respondents are three former Hazelwood East students who were staff members of *Spectrum*, the school newspaper. They contend that school officials violated their First Amendment rights by deleting two pages of articles from the May 13, 1983, issue of *Spectrum*.

Spectrum was written and edited by the Journalism II class at Hazelwood East. The newspaper was published every three weeks or so during the 1982-1983 school year. More than 4,500 copies of the newspaper were distributed during that year to students, school personnel, and members of the community.

The Board of Education allocated funds from its annual budget for the printing of *Spectrum*. These funds were supplemented by proceeds from sales of the newspaper. The printing expenses during the 1982-1983 school year totaled $4,668.50; revenue from sales was $1,166.84. The other costs associated with the newspaper - such as supplies, textbooks, and a portion of the journalism teacher's salary - were borne entirely by the Board.

The Journalism II course was taught by Robert Stergos for most of the 1982-1983 academic year. Stergos left Hazelwood East to take a job in private industry on April 29, 1983, when the May 13 edition of *Spectrum* was nearing completion, and petitioner Emerson took his place as newspaper adviser for the remaining weeks of the term.

The practice at Hazelwood East during the spring 1983 semester was for the journalism teacher to submit page proofs of each *Spectrum* issue to Principal Reynolds for his review prior to publication. On May 10, Emerson delivered the proofs of the May 13 edition to Reynolds, who objected to two of the articles scheduled to appear in that edition. One of the stories described three Hazelwood East students' experiences with pregnancy; the other discussed the impact of divorce on students at the school.

Reynolds was concerned that, although the pregnancy story used false names "to keep the identity of these girls a secret," the pregnant students still might be identifiable from the text. He also believed that the article's references to sexual activity and birth control were inappropriate for some of the younger students at the school. In addition, Reynolds was concerned that a student identified by name in the divorce story had complained that her father "wasn't spending enough time with my mom, my sister and I" prior to the divorce, "was always out of town on business or out late playing cards with the guys," and "always argued about everything" with her mother. Reynolds believed that the student's parents should have been given an opportunity to respond to these remarks or to consent to their publication. He was unaware that Emerson had deleted the student's name from the final version of the article.

Reynolds believed that there was no time to make the necessary changes in the stories before the scheduled press run and that the newspaper would not appear before the end of the school year if printing were delayed to any significant extent. He concluded that his only options under the circumstances were to publish a four-page newspaper instead of the planned six-page newspaper, eliminating the two pages on which the offending stories appeared, or to publish no newspaper at all. Accordingly, he directed Emerson to withhold from publication the two pages containing the stories on pregnancy and divorce. He informed his superiors of the decision, and they concurred.

[The students] subsequently commenced this action in the United States District Court for the Eastern District of Missouri seeking a declaration that their First Amendment rights had been violated, injunctive relief [a court order stopping an action], and monetary damages. After a bench trial, the District Court denied an injunction, holding that no First Amendment violation had occurred.

The District Court concluded that school officials may impose restraints on students' speech in activities that are "'an integral part of the school's educational function'" - including the publication of a school-sponsored newspaper by a journalism class - so long as their decision has "'a substantial and reasonable basis.'" The court found that Principal Reynolds' concern that the pregnant student's anonymity would be lost and their privacy invaded was "legitimate and reasonable," given "the small number of pregnant students at Hazelwood East and several identifying characteristics that were disclosed in the article." The court held that Reynolds' action was also justified "to avoid the impression that [the school] endorses the sexual norms of the subjects" and to shield younger students from exposure to unsuitable material. The deletion of the article on divorce was seen by the court as a reasonable response to the invasion of privacy concerns raised by the named student's remarks. Because the article did not indicate that the student's parents had been offered an opportunity to respond to her allegations, said the court, there was cause for "serious doubt that the article complied with the rules of fairness which are standard in the field of journalism and which were covered in the textbook used in the Journalism II class." Furthermore, the court concluded that Reynolds was justified in deleting two full pages of the newspaper, instead of deleting only the pregnancy and divorce stories or requiring that those stories be modified to address his concerns, based on his "reasonable belief that he had to make an immediate decision and that there was no time to make modifications to the articles in question."

The Court of Appeals for the Eighth Circuit reversed. The court held at the outset that *Spectrum* was not only "a part of the school adopted curriculum," but also a public forum, because the newspaper was "intended to be and operated as a conduit for student viewpoint." The court then concluded that *Spectrum's* status as a public forum precluded school officials from censoring its contents except when "'necessary to avoid material and substantial interference with school work or discipline . . . or the rights of others.'"

The Court of Appeals found "no evidence in the record that the principal could have reasonably forecast that the censored articles or any materials in the censored articles would have materially disrupted classwork or given rise to substantial disorder in the school." School officials were entitled to censor the articles on the ground that they invaded the rights of others, according to the court, only if publication of the articles could have resulted in tort [civil] liability to the school. The court concluded that no tort action for libel or invasion of privacy could have been maintained against the school by the subjects of the two articles or by their families. Accordingly, the court held that school officials had violated [the students'] First Amendment rights by deleting the two pages of the newspaper.

We granted certiorari [agreed to hear the case], and we now reverse.

Students in the public schools do not "shed their constitutional rights to freedom of speech or expression at the schoolhouse gate." They cannot be punished merely for expressing their personal views on the school premises - whether "in the cafeteria, or on the playing field, or on the campus during the authorized hours," unless school authorities have reason to believe that such expression will "substantially interfere with the work of the school or impinge upon the rights of other students."

We have nonetheless recognized that the First Amendment rights of students in the public schools "are not automatically coextensive with the rights of adults in other settings," and must be "applied in light of the special characteristics of the school environment." A school need not tolerate student speech that is inconsistent with its "basic educational mission," even though the government could not censor similar speech outside the school. Accordingly, we held in *Fraser* that a student could be disciplined for having delivered a speech that was "sexually explicit" but not legally obscene at an official school assembly, because the school was entitled to "disassociate itself" from the speech in a manner that would demonstrate to others that such vulgarity is "wholly inconsistent with the 'fundamental values' of public school education." We thus recognized that "[t]he determination of what manner of speech in the classroom or in school assembly is inappropriate properly rests with the school board," rather than with the federal courts. It is in this context that [the students'] First Amendment claims must be considered.

We deal first with the question whether *Spectrum* may appropriately be characterized as a forum for public expression. The public schools do not possess all of the attributes of streets, parks, and other traditional public forums that "time out of mind, have been used for purposes of assembly, communicating thoughts between citizens, and discussing public questions." Hence, school facilities may be deemed to be public forums only if school authorities have "by policy or by practice" opened those facilities "for indiscriminate use by the general public," or by some segment of the public, such as student organizations. If the facilities have instead been reserved for other intended purposes, "communicative or otherwise," then no public forum has been created, and school officials may impose reasonable restrictions on the speech of students, teachers, and other members of the school community. "The government does not create a public forum by inaction or by permitting limited discourse, but only by intentionally opening a nontraditional forum for public discourse."

The policy of school officials toward *Spectrum* was reflected in Hazelwood School Board Policy 348.51 and the Hazelwood East Curriculum Guide. Board Policy 348.51 provided that "[s]chool sponsored publications are developed within the adopted curriculum and its educational implications in regular classroom activities." The Hazelwood East Curriculum Guide described the Journalism II course as a "laboratory situation in which the students publish the school newspaper applying skills they have learned in Journalism I." The lessons that were to be learned from the Journalism II course, according to the Curriculum Guide, included development of journalistic skills under deadline pressure, "the legal, moral, and ethical restrictions imposed upon journalists within the school community," and "responsibility and acceptance of criticism for articles of opinion." Journalism II was taught by a faculty member during regular class hours. Students received grades and academic credit for their performance in the course.

School officials did not deviate in practice from their policy that production of *Spectrum* was to be part of the educational curriculum and a "regular classroom activit[y]." The District Court found that Robert Stergos, the journalism teacher during most of the 1982-1983 school year, "both had the authority to exercise and in fact exercised a great deal of control over *Spectrum*." For example, Stergos selected the editors of the newspaper, scheduled publication dates, decided the number of pages for each issue, assigned story ideas to class members, advised students on the development of their stories, reviewed the use of quotations, edited stories, selected and edited the letters to the editor, and dealt with the printing company. Many of these decisions were made without consultation with the Journalism II students. The District Court thus found it "clear that Mr. Stergos was the final authority with respect to almost every aspect of the production and publication of *Spectrum*, including its content." Moreover, after each *Spectrum* issue had been finally approved by Stergos or his successor, the issue still had to be reviewed by Principal Reynolds prior to publication. [The students'] assertion that they had believed that they could publish "practically anything" in *Spectrum* was therefore dismissed by the District Court as simply "not credible." These factual findings are amply supported by the record, and were not rejected as clearly erroneous by the Court of Appeals.

The evidence relied upon by the Court of Appeals in finding *Spectrum* to be a public forum, is equivocal at best. For example, Board Policy 348.51, which stated in part that "[s]chool sponsored student publications will not restrict free expression or diverse viewpoints within the rules of responsible journalism," also stated that such publications were "developed within the adopted curriculum and its educational implications." One might reasonably infer from the full text of Policy 348.51 that school officials retained ultimate control over what constituted "responsible journalism" in a school-sponsored newspaper. Although the Statement of Policy published in the September 14, 1982, issue of *Spectrum* declared that "*Spectrum*, as a student-press publication, accepts all rights implied by the First Amendment," this statement, understood in the context of the paper's role in the school's curriculum, suggests at most that the administration will not interfere with the students' exercise of those First Amendment rights that attend the publication of a school-sponsored newspaper. It does not reflect an intent to expand those rights by converting a curricular newspaper into a public forum. Finally, that students were permitted to exercise some authority over the contents of *Spectrum* was fully consistent with the Curriculum Guide objective of teaching the Journalism II students "leadership responsibilities as issue and page editors." A decision to teach leadership skills in the context of a classroom activity hardly implies a decision to relinquish school control over that activity. In sum, the evidence relied upon by the Court of Appeals fails to demonstrate the "clear intent to create a public forum," that existed in cases in which we found public forums to have been created. School officials did not evince either "by policy or by practice," any intent to open the pages of *Spectrum* to "indiscriminate use," by its student reporters and editors, or by the student body generally. Instead, they "reserve[d] the forum for its intended purpos[e]," as a supervised learning experience for journalism students. Accordingly, school officials were entitled to regulate the contents of *Spectrum* in any reasonable manner. It is this standard, rather than our decision in *Tinker*, that governs this case.

The question whether the First Amendment requires a school to tolerate particular student speech - the question that we addressed in Tinker - is different from the question whether the First Amendment requires a school affirmatively to promote particular student speech. The former question addresses educators' ability to silence a student's personal expression that happens to occur on the school premises. The latter question concerns educators' authority over school-sponsored publications, theatrical productions, and other expressive activities that students, parents, and members of the public might reasonably perceive to bear the imprimatur of the school. These activities may fairly be characterized as part of the school curriculum, whether or not they occur in a traditional classroom setting, so long as they are supervised by faculty members and designed to impart particular knowledge or skills to student participants and audiences.

Educators are entitled to exercise greater control over this second form of student expression to assure that participants learn whatever lessons the activity is designed to teach, that readers or listeners are not exposed to material that may be inappropriate for their level of maturity, and that the views of the individual speaker are not erroneously attributed to the school. Hence, a school may in its capacity as publisher of a school newspaper or producer of a school play "disassociate itself," not only from speech that would "substantially interfere with [its] work . . . or impinge upon the rights of other students," but also from speech that is, for example, ungrammatical, poorly written, inadequately researched, biased or prejudiced, vulgar or profane, or unsuitable for immature audiences. A school must be able to set high standards for the student speech that is disseminated under its auspices - standards that may be higher than those demanded by some newspaper publishers or theatrical producers in the "real" world - and may refuse to disseminate student speech that does not meet those standards. In addition, a school must be able to take into account the emotional maturity of the intended audience in determining whether to disseminate student speech on potentially sensitive topics, which might range from the existence of Santa Claus in an elementary school setting to the particulars of teenage sexual activity in a high school setting. A school must also retain the authority to refuse to sponsor student speech that might reasonably be perceived to advocate drug or alcohol use, irresponsible sex, or conduct otherwise inconsistent with "the shared values of a civilized social order," or to associate the school with any position other than neutrality on matters of political controversy. Otherwise, the schools would be unduly constrained from fulfilling their role as "a principal instrument in awakening the child to cultural values, in preparing him for later professional training, and in helping him to adjust normally to his environment."

Accordingly, we conclude that the standard articulated in *Tinker* for determining when a school may punish student expression need not also be the standard for determining when a school may refuse to lend its name and resources to the dissemination of student expression. Instead, we hold that educators do not offend the First Amendment by exercising editorial control over the style and content of student speech in school-sponsored expressive activities so long as their actions are reasonably related to legitimate pedagogical concerns.

This standard is consistent with our oft-expressed view that the education of the Nation's youth is primarily the responsibility of parents, teachers, and state and local school officials, and not of federal judges. It is only when the decision to censor a school-sponsored publication, theatrical production, or other vehicle of student expression has no valid educational purpose that the First Amendment is so "directly and sharply implicate[d]," as to require judicial intervention to protect students' constitutional rights.

We also conclude that Principal Reynolds acted reasonably in requiring the deletion from the May 13 issue of *Spectrum* of the pregnancy article, the divorce article, and the remaining articles that were to appear on the same pages of the newspaper.

The initial paragraph of the pregnancy article declared that "[a]ll names have been changed to keep the identity of these girls a secret." The principal concluded that the students' anonymity was not adequately protected, however, given the other identifying information in the article and the small number of pregnant students at the school. Indeed, a teacher at the school credibly testified that she could positively identify at least one of the girls and possibly all three. It is likely that many students at Hazelwood East would have been at least as successful in identifying the girls. Reynolds therefore could reasonably have feared that the article violated whatever pledge of anonymity had been given to the pregnant students. In addition, he could reasonably have been concerned that the article was not sufficiently sensitive to the privacy interests of the students' boyfriends and parents, who were discussed in the article but who were given no opportunity to consent to its publication or to offer a response. The article did not contain graphic accounts of sexual activity. The girls did comment in the article, however, concerning their sexual histories and their use or nonuse of birth control. It was not unreasonable for the principal to have concluded that such frank talk was inappropriate in a school-sponsored publication distributed to 14-year-old freshmen and presumably taken home to be read by students' even younger brothers and sisters.

The student who was quoted by name in the version of the divorce article seen by Principal Reynolds made comments sharply critical of her father. The principal could reasonably have concluded that an individual publicly identified as an inattentive parent - indeed, as one who chose "playing cards with the guys" over home and family - was entitled to an opportunity to defend himself as a matter of journalistic fairness. These concerns were shared by both of *Spectrum*'s faculty advisers for the 1982-1983 school year, who testified that they would not have allowed the article to be printed without deletion of the student's name.

Principal Reynolds testified credibly at trial that, at the time that he reviewed the proofs of the May 13 issue during an extended telephone conversation with Emerson, he believed that there was no time to make any changes in the articles, and that the newspaper had to be printed immediately or not at all. It is true that Reynolds did not verify whether the necessary modifications could still have been made in the articles, and that Emerson did not volunteer the information that printing could be delayed until the changes were made. We nonetheless agree with the District Court that the decision to excise the two pages containing the problematic articles was reasonable given the particular circumstances of this case. These circumstances included the very recent replacement of Stergos by Emerson, who may not have been entirely familiar with *Spectrum* editorial and production procedures, and the pressure felt by Reynolds to make an immediate decision so that students would not be deprived of the newspaper altogether.

In sum, we cannot reject as unreasonable Principal Reynolds' conclusion that neither the pregnancy article nor the divorce article was suitable for publication in *Spectrum*. Reynolds could reasonably have concluded that the students who had written and edited these articles had not sufficiently mastered those portions of the Journalism II curriculum that pertained to the treatment of controversial issues and personal attacks, the need to protect the privacy of individuals whose most intimate concerns are to be revealed in the newspaper, and "the legal, moral, and ethical restrictions imposed upon journalists within [a] school community" that includes adolescent subjects and readers. Finally, we conclude that the principal's decision to delete two pages of *Spectrum*, rather than to delete only the offending articles or to require that they be modified, was reasonable under the circumstances as he understood them. Accordingly, no violation of First Amendment rights occurred.

The judgment of the Court of Appeals for the Eighth Circuit is therefore reversed.

Prayers At Graduation
Lee v. Weisman

On June 29, 1989 at the invitation of Robert E. Lee, Principal of the Nathan Bishop Middle School in Providence, Rhode Island, a local clergyman, Rabbi Leslie Gutterman, was asked to offer invocation and benediction prayers as part of the school's graduation ceremony. The prayers were to be structured in accordance with the National Conference of Christians and Jews' "Guidelines For Civic Occasions," which recommended that at nonsectarian civic ceremonies, such as public school graduations, prayers be composed with elements of inclusiveness and sensitivity.

Deborah Weisman, a fourteen-year-old graduating senior, objected to the inclusion of any prayer at the ceremonies. Four days before the graduation Deborah's father, Daniel, brought suit in Federal District Court to prohibit the prayers, claiming they violated the First Amendment's Establishment Clause. The District Court, citing a lack of adequate time to consider the matter, denied the Weismans' request. This prayer was said at the graduation: *O God, we are grateful to You for having endowed us with the capacity for learning which we have celebrated on this joyous commencement.*

The Weismans continued their suit against Principal Lee to prevent any future graduation prayers in Providence schools. This time the U.S. District Court held for the Weismans, finding that the prayers were an impermissible governmental endorsement of religion. Lee appealed to the U.S. Court of Appeals, which affirmed the decision. Lee then appealed to the United States Supreme Court.

Oral arguments were heard in *Lee v. Weisman* on November 6, 1991 and the 5-4 decision of the Court was announced on June 24, 1992 by Associate Justice Anthony Kennedy.

The Weisman Court

Chief Justice William Rehnquist
Appointed Chief Justice by President Reagan
Appointed Associate Justice by President Nixon
Served 1971 -

Associate Justice Byron White
Appointed by President Kennedy
Served 1962 - 1993

Associate Justice Harry Blackmun
Appointed by President Nixon
Served 1970 - 1994

Associate Justice John Paul Stevens
Appointed by President Ford
Served 1975 -

Associate Justice Sandra Day O'Connor
Appointed by President Reagan
Served 1981 -

Associate Justice Antonin Scalia
Appointed by President Reagan
Served 1986 -

Associate Justice Anthony Kennedy
Appointed by President Reagan
Served 1988 -

Associate Justice David Souter
Appointed by President Bush
Served 1990 -

Associate Justice Clarence Thomas
Appointed by President Bush
Served 1991 -

The unedited text of *Lee v. Weisman* can be found on page 577, volume 512 of *U.S. Reports*. Our edited text follows.

LEE v. WEISMAN
June 24, 1992

JUSTICE ANTHONY KENNEDY: School principals in the public school system of the city of Providence, Rhode Island, are permitted to invite members of the clergy to offer invocation and benediction prayers as part of the formal graduation ceremonies for middle schools and for high schools. The question before us is whether including clerical members who offer prayers as part of the official school graduation ceremony is consistent with the Religion Clauses of the First Amendment, provisions the Fourteenth Amendment makes applicable with full force to the States and their school districts.

Deborah Weisman graduated from Nathan Bishop Middle School, a public school in Providence, at a formal ceremony in June 1989. She was about fourteen years old. For many years it has been the policy of the Providence School Committee and the Superintendent of Schools to permit principals to invite members of the clergy to give invocations and benedictions at middle school and high school graduations. Many, but not all, of the principals elected to include prayers as part of the graduation ceremonies. Acting for himself and his daughter, Deborah's father, Daniel Weisman, objected to any prayers at Deborah's middle school graduation, but to no avail. The school principal, petitioner Robert E. Lee, invited a rabbi to deliver prayers at the graduation exercises for Deborah's class. Rabbi Leslie Gutterman, of the Temple Beth El in Providence, accepted.

. . . . Rabbi Gutterman's prayers were as follows:

"INVOCATION

"God of the Free, Hope of the Brave:

"For the legacy of America where diversity is celebrated and the rights of minorities are protected, we thank You. May these young men and women grow up to enrich it.

"For the liberty of America, we thank You. May these new graduates grow up to guard it.

"For the political process of America in which all its citizens may participate, for its court system where all may seek justice we thank You. May those we honor this morning always turn to it in trust.

"For the destiny of America we thank You. May the graduates of Nathan Bishop Middle School so live that they might help to share it.

"May our aspirations for our country and for these young people, who are our hope for the future, be richly fulfilled.

AMEN"

"BENEDICTION

"O God, we are grateful to You for having endowed us with the capacity for learning which we have celebrated on this joyous commencement.

"Happy families give thanks for seeing their children achieve an important milestone. Send Your blessings upon the teachers and administrators who helped prepare them.

"The graduates now need strength and guidance for the future, help them to understand that we are not complete with academic knowledge alone. We must each strive to fulfill what You require of us all: To do justly, to love mercy, to walk humbly.

"We give thanks to You, Lord, for keeping us alive, sustaining us and allowing us to reach this special, happy occasion.

AMEN"

. . . . The school board (and the United States, which supports it as *amicus curiae* [friend of the Court]) argued that these short prayers and others like them at graduation exercises are of profound meaning to many students and parents throughout this country who consider that due respect and acknowledgment for divine guidance and for the deepest spiritual aspirations of our people ought to be expressed at an event as important in life as a graduation. We assume this to be so in addressing the difficult case now before us, for the significance of the prayers lies also at the heart of Daniel and Deborah Weisman's case.

Deborah's graduation was held on the premises of Nathan Bishop Middle School on June 29, 1989. Four days before the ceremony, Daniel Weisman . . . sought a temporary restraining order in the United States District Court for the District of Rhode Island to prohibit school officials from including an invocation or benediction in the graduation ceremony. The court denied the motion for lack of adequate time to consider it. Deborah and her family attended the graduation, where the prayers were recited. In July 1989,

Daniel Weisman filed an amended complaint seeking a permanent injunction [court order stopping an action] barring petitioners, various officials of the Providence public schools, from inviting the clergy to deliver invocations and benedictions at future graduations. . . . Deborah Weisman is enrolled as a student at Classical High School in Providence and from the record it appears likely, if not certain, that an invocation and benediction will be conducted at her high school graduation.

. . . . The District Court held that petitioners' practice of including invocations and benedictions in public school graduations violated the Establishment Clause of the First Amendment, and it enjoined [prohibited] petitioners from continuing the practice. . . .

On appeal, the United States Court of Appeals for the First Circuit affirmed [upheld]. . . . We granted certiorari [agreed to hear the case], and now affirm.

These dominant facts mark and control the confines of our decision: State officials direct the performance of a formal religious exercise at promotional and graduation ceremonies for secondary schools. Even for those students who object to the religious exercise, their attendance and participation in the state-sponsored religious activity are in a fair and real sense obligatory, though the school district does not require attendance as a condition for receipt of the diploma.

. . . . The government involvement with religious activity in this case is pervasive, to the point of creating a state-sponsored and state-directed religious exercise in a public school. Conducting this formal religious observance conflicts with settled rules pertaining to prayer exercises for students, and that suffices to determine the question before us.

The principle that government may accommodate the free exercise of religion does not supersede the fundamental limitations imposed by the Establishment Clause. It is beyond dispute that, at a minimum, the Constitution guarantees that government may not coerce anyone to support or participate in religion or its exercise, or otherwise act in a way which "establishes a [state] religion or religious faith, or tends to do so." The State's involvement in the school prayers challenged today violates these central principles.

That involvement is as troubling as it is undenied. A school official, the principal, decided that an invocation and a benediction should be given; this is a choice attributable to the State, and from a constitutional perspective it is as if a state statute decreed that the prayers must occur. The principal chose the religious participant, here a rabbi, and that choice is also attributable to the State. . . .

The State's role did not end with the decision to include a prayer and with the choice of clergyman. Principal Lee provided Rabbi Gutterman with a copy of the "Guidelines for Civic Occasions," and advised him that his prayers should be nonsectarian. Through these means the principal directed and controlled the content of the prayers. . . . It is a cornerstone principle of our Establishment Clause jurisprudence that "it is no part of the business of government to compose official prayers for any group of the American people to recite as a part of a religious program carried on by government," and that is what the school officials attempted to do.

. . . . The First Amendment's Religion Clauses mean that religious beliefs and religious expression are too precious to be either proscribed or prescribed by the State. The design of the Constitution is that preservation and transmission of religious beliefs and worship is a responsibility and a choice committed to the private sphere, which itself is promised freedom to pursue that mission. It must not be forgotten then, that while concern must be given to define the protection granted to an objector or a dissenting nonbeliever, these same Clauses exist to protect religion from government interference. . . .

These concerns have particular application in the case of school officials, whose effort to monitor prayer will be perceived by the students as inducing a participation they might otherwise reject. Though the efforts of the school officials in this case to find common ground appear to have been a good-faith attempt to recognize the common aspects of religions and not the divisive ones, our precedents do not permit school officials to assist in composing prayers as an incident to a formal exercise for their students. . . .

The degree of school involvement here made it clear that the graduation prayers bore the imprint of the State and thus put school-age children who objected in an untenable position. . . .

The injury caused by the government's action, and the reason why Daniel and Deborah Weisman object to it, is that the State, in a school setting, in effect required participation in a religious exercise. It is, we concede, a brief exercise during which the individual can concentrate on joining its message, meditate on her own religion, or let her mind wander. But the embarrassment and the intrusion of the religious exercise cannot be refuted by arguing that these prayers, and similar ones to be said in the future, are of a *de minimis* [insignificant] character. To do so would be an affront to the rabbi who offered them and to all those for whom the prayers were an essential and profound recognition of divine authority. And for the same reason, we think that the intrusion is greater than the two minutes or so of time consumed for prayers like these. Assuming, as we must, that the prayers were offensive to the student and the parent who now object, the intrusion was both real and, in the context of a secondary school, a violation of the objectors' rights. That the intrusion was in the course of promulgating religion that sought to be civic or nonsectarian rather than pertaining to one sect does not lessen the offense or isolation to the objectors. At best it narrows their number, at worst increases their sense of isolation and affront.

. . . . The sole question presented is whether a religious exercise may be conducted at a graduation ceremony in circumstances where, as we have found, young graduates who object are induced to conform. No holding by this Court suggests that a school can persuade or compel a student to participate in a religious exercise. That is being done here, and it is forbidden by the Establishment Clause of the First Amendment.

For the reasons we have stated, the judgment of the Court of Appeals is affirmed.

Guns In Schools
United States v. Lopez

On March 10, 1992, Alfonso Lopez, Jr., a twelfth-grade student at Edison High School in San Antonio, Texas, was arrested for carrying a concealed .38 caliber handgun to school. A Federal Grand Jury indicted Lopez for violating the Federal Gun-Free School Zone Act.

The Federal Gun-Free School Zone Act was passed in 1990 by the United States Congress making it a federal offense for any individual to knowingly possess a firearm in a school zone. "School Zone" was defined in the Act as being either on the grounds of, or within 1,000 feet from, a public, parochial or private school. For the authority to enact this law the Congress relied on the Constitution's Commerce Clause.

Lopez asked a Federal District Court to dismiss the indictment against him on the grounds that the Gun-Free School Zone Act was unconstitutional. The Congress, Lopez argued, had no legal authority under the Constitution's Commerce Clause to legislate control over public schools. The District Court rejected this argument. Lopez was tried, convicted, and sentenced to six months' imprisonment for violating the Gun Free School Zone Act. Lopez appealed his conviction to the United States Court of Appeals, arguing again that Congress had exceeded their Constitutional authority when they passed the Gun-Free School Zone Act. On September 15, 1993 the U.S. Court of Appeals found for Lopez and reversed his conviction. The U.S. Justice Department appealed to the U.S. Supreme Court.

Oral arguments were heard in *United States v. Lopez* on November 8, 1994 and the 5-4 decision of the United States Supreme Court was announced on April 26, 1995 by Chief Justice William Rehnquist.

The Lopez Court

Chief Justice William Rehnquist
Appointed Chief Justice by President Reagan
Appointed Associate Justice by President Nixon
Served 1971 -

Associate Justice John Paul Stevens
Appointed by President Ford
Served 1975 -

Associate Justice Sandra Day O'Connor
Appointed by President Reagan
Served 1981 -

Associate Justice Antonin Scalia
Appointed by President Reagan
Served 1986 -

Associate Justice Anthony Kennedy
Appointed by President Reagan
Served 1988 -

Associate Justice David Souter
Appointed by President Bush
Served 1990 -

Associate Justice Clarence Thomas
Appointed by President Bush
Served 1991 -

Associate Justice Ruth Bader Ginsberg
Appointed by President Clinton
Served 1993 -

Associate Justice Stephen Breyer
Appointed by President Clinton
Served 1994 -

The unedited text of *United States v. Lopez* can be found in volume 514 of *United States Reports*. Our edited text follows.

UNITED STATES v. LOPEZ
April 26, 1995

CHIEF JUSTICE WILLIAM REHNQUIST: In the Gun-Free School Zones Act of 1990, Congress made it a federal offense "for any individual knowingly to possess a firearm at a place that the individual knows, or has reasonable cause to believe, is a school zone." The Act neither regulates a commercial activity nor contains a requirement that the possession be connected in any way to interstate commerce. We hold that the Act exceeds the authority of Congress "[t]o regulate Commerce . . . among the several States. . . ."

On March 10, 1992, respondent [Alfonso Lopez, Jr.], who was then a 12th-grade student, arrived at Edison High School in San Antonio, Texas, carrying a concealed .38 caliber handgun and five bullets. Acting upon an anonymous tip, school authorities confronted [Lopez], who admitted that he was carrying the weapon. He was arrested and charged under Texas law with firearm possession on school premises. The next day, the state charges were dismissed after federal agents charged [him] . . . with violating the Gun-Free School Zones Act of 1990.

A federal grand jury indicted [charged Lopez] on one count of knowing possession of a firearm at a school zone, in violation of [the Gun-Free School Zones Act]. [Lopez] moved to dismiss his federal indictment on the ground that [the Act] "is unconstitutional as it is beyond the power of Congress to legislate control over our public schools." The District Court denied the motion, concluding that [the Gun-Free School Zones Act] "is a constitutional exercise of Congress' well-defined power to regulate activities in and affecting commerce, and the 'business of elementary, mid-

dle and high schools . . . affects interstate commerce.'"
[Lopez] waived his right to a jury trial. The District Court
conducted a bench trial, found him guilty of violating [the
Act], and sentenced him to six months' imprisonment and
two years' supervised release.

On appeal, [Lopez] challenged his conviction based on his
claim that [the Gun-Free School Zones Act] exceeded
Congress' power to legislate under the Commerce Clause.
The Court of Appeals for the Fifth Circuit agreed and reversed [his] conviction. It held that, in light of what it characterized as insufficient congressional findings and legislative history, "[the Gun-Free School Zones Act], in the full
reach of its terms, is invalid as beyond the power of Congress under the Commerce Clause." Because of the importance of the issue, we granted certiorari [agreed to hear
the case], and we now affirm [uphold].

. . . . [The Gun-Free School Zones Act] is a criminal statute
that by its terms has nothing to do with "commerce" or
any sort of economic enterprise, however broadly one
might define those terms. [The Act] is not an essential part
of a larger regulation of economic activity, in which the
regulatory scheme could be undercut unless the intrastate
activity were regulated. It cannot, therefore, be sustained
under our cases upholding regulations of activities that arise
out of or are connected with a commercial transaction,
which viewed in the aggregate, substantially affects interstate commerce.

Second, [the Gun-Free School Zones Act] contains no ju-
risdictional element which would ensure, through case-by-
case inquiry, that the firearm possession in question affects
interstate commerce. For example, in *United States v. Bass*,
the Court interpreted [the U.S. Code] which made it a
crime for a felon to "receiv[e], posses[s], or transpor[t] in

commerce or affecting commerce . . . any firearm." The court interpreted the possession component of [this law] to require an additional nexus to interstate commerce both because the statute was ambiguous and because "unless Congress conveys its purpose clearly, it will not be deemed to have significantly changed the federal-state balance." . . .

Although as part of our independent evaluation of constitutionality under the Commerce Clause we of course consider legislative findings, and indeed even congressional committee findings, regarding effect on interstate commerce, the Government concedes that "[n]either the statute nor its legislative history contain[s] express congressional findings regarding the effects upon interstate commerce of gun possession in a school zone." We agree with the Government that Congress normally is not required to make formal findings as to the substantial burdens that an activity has on interstate commerce. But to the extent that congressional findings would enable us to evaluate the legislative judgment that the activity in question substantially affected interstate commerce, even though no such substantial effect was visible to the naked eye, they are lacking here.

The Government argues that Congress has accumulated institutional expertise regarding the regulation of firearms through previous enactments. We agree, however, with the Fifth Circuit that importation of previous findings to justify [the Gun-Free School Zones Act] is especially inappropriate here because the "prior federal enactments or Congressional findings [do not] speak to the subject matter of [the Act] or its relationship to interstate commerce. Indeed, [the Gun-Free School Zones Act] plows thoroughly new ground and represents a sharp break with the long-standing pattern of federal firearms legislation."

The Government's essential contention . . . is that we may determine here that [the Gun-Free School Zones Act] is valid because possession of a firearm in a local school zone does indeed substantially affect interstate commerce. The Government argues that possession of a firearm in a school zone may result in violent crime and that violent crime can be expected to affect the functioning of the national economy in two ways. First, the costs of violent crime are substantial, and, through the mechanism of insurance, those costs are spread throughout the population. Second, violent crime reduces the willingness of individuals to travel to areas within the country that are perceived to be unsafe. Government also argues that the presence of guns in schools poses a substantial threat to the educational process by threatening the learning environment. A handicapped educational process, in turn, will result in a less productive citizenry. That, in turn, would have an adverse effect on the Nation's economic well-being. As a result, the Government argues that Congress could rationally have concluded that [the Gun-Free School Zones Act] substantially affects interstate commerce.

We pause to consider the implications of the Government's arguments. The Government admits, under its "costs of crime" reasoning, that Congress could regulate not only all violent crime, but all activities that might lead to violent crime, regardless of how tenuously they relate to interstate commerce. Similarly, under the Government's "national productivity" reasoning, Congress could regulate any activity that it found was related to the economic productivity of individual citizens: family law (including marriage, divorce, and child custody), for example. Under the theories that the Government presents in support of [the Gun-Free School Zones Act], it is difficult to perceive any limitation on federal power, even in areas such as criminal law enforcement or education where States historically have been sovereign.

Thus, if we were to accept the Government's arguments, we are hard-pressed to posit any activity by an individual that Congress is without power to regulate.

. . . . [I]f Congress can, pursuant to its Commerce Clause power, regulate activities that adversely affect the learning environment, then . . . it also can regulate the educational process directly. Congress could determine that a school's curriculum has a "significant" effect on the extent of classroom learning. As a result, Congress could mandate a federal curriculum for local elementary and secondary schools because what is taught in local schools has a significant "effect on classroom learning," and that, in turn, has a substantial effect on interstate commerce.

. . . . We do not doubt that Congress has authority under the Commerce Clause to regulate numerous commercial activities that substantially affect interstate commerce and also affect the educational process. That authority, though broad, does not include the authority to regulate each and every aspect of local schools.

. . . . The possession of a gun in a local school zone is in no sense an economic activity that might, through repetition elsewhere, substantially affect any sort of interstate commerce. [Lopez] was a local student at a local school; there is no indication that he had recently moved in interstate commerce, and there is no requirement that his possession of the firearm have any concrete tie to interstate commerce.

To uphold the Government's contentions here, we would have to pile inference upon inference in a manner that would bid fair to convert congressional authority under the Commerce Clause to a general police power of the sort retained by the States. Admittedly, some of our prior cases have taken long steps down that road, giving great deference to congressional action. The broad language in these opinions has suggested the possibility of additional expansion, but we decline here to proceed any further. To do so would require us to conclude that the Constitution's enumeration of powers does not presuppose something not enumerated, and that there never will be a distinction between what is truly national and what is truly local. This we are unwilling to do.

For the foregoing reasons the judgment of the Court of Appeals is affirmed.

Student Athlete Drug Testing
Vernonia Schools v. Acton

Student Athlete Drug Testing Authorization Form
I _____ authorize the Vernonia School District to conduct a test on a urine specimen which I provide to test for drug and/or alcohol use.

In 1989 the Vernonia, Oregon School District, to counteract drug-related disciplinary problems of "epidemic proportions," implemented a Student Athlete Drug Testing Policy. All students signing up for athletic teams were required to sign a Drug Testing Authorization Form and their parents were required to sign a Drug Testing Consent Form. A urine specimen was required at the start of the season and, during the season, students were subject to random drug tests.

In the fall of 1991 James Acton, a seventh-grade student attending a Vernonia grade school, was refused participation in the football program when he and his parents, Wayne and Judy, refused to authorize and consent to a drug test. The Actons filed suit in U.S. District Court, seeking to overturn the Student Athlete Drug Testing Policy on the grounds that the Vernonia District's suspicionless drug tests violated James' Fourth Amendment protection against unreasonable searches. On May 7, 1992 the District Court upheld the constitutionality of the Vernonia School District's Drug Testing Policy. The Acton Family appealed for a reversal to the U.S. Court of Appeals. On May 5, 1994 that Court, holding that the Policy violated the Fourth Amendment, found for the Actons. The Vernonia School District appealed to the United States Supreme Court.

Oral arguments were heard in *Vernonia Schools v. Acton* on March 28, 1995 and the 6-3 decision was announced on June 26, 1995 by Associate Justice Antonin Scalia.

The Vernonia Court

Chief Justice William Rehnquist
Appointed Chief Justice by President Reagan
Appointed Associate Justice by President Nixon
Served 1971 -

Associate Justice John Paul Stevens
Appointed by President Ford
Served 1975 -

Associate Justice Sandra Day O'Connor
Appointed by President Reagan
Served 1981 -

Associate Justice Antonin Scalia
Appointed by President Reagan
Served 1986 -

Associate Justice Anthony Kennedy
Appointed by President Reagan
Served 1988 -

Associate Justice David Souter
Appointed by President Bush
Served 1990 -

Associate Justice Clarence Thomas
Appointed by President Bush
Served 1991 -

Associate Justice Ruth Bader Ginsberg
Appointed by President Clinton
Served 1993 -

Associate Justice Stephen Breyer
Appointed by President Clinton
Served 1994 -

The unedited text of *Vernonia Schools v. Acton* can be found in volume 515 of *United States Reports*. Our edited text follows.

VERNONIA SCHOOLS v. ACTON
June 26, 1995

JUSTICE ANTONIN SCALIA: The Student Athlete Drug Policy adopted by School District 47J in the town of Vernonia, Oregon, authorizes random urinalysis drug testing of students who participate in the District's school athletics programs. We granted certiorari [agreed to hear the case] to decide whether this violates the Fourth and Fourteenth Amendments to the United States Constitution.

Petitioner Vernonia School District 47J (District) operates one high school and three grade schools in the logging community of Vernonia, Oregon. As elsewhere in small-town America, school sports play a prominent role in the town's life, and student athletes are admired in their schools and in the community.

Drugs had not been a major problem in Vernonia schools. In the mid-to-late 1980's, however, teachers and administrators observed a sharp increase in drug use. Students began to speak out about their attraction to the drug culture, and to boast that there was nothing the school could do about it. Along with more drugs came more disciplinary problems. Between 1988 and 1989 the number of disciplinary referrals in Vernonia schools rose to more than twice the number reported in the early 1980's, and several students were suspended. Students became increasingly rude during class; outbursts of profane language became common.

Not only were student athletes included among the drug users but, as the District Court found, athletes were the leaders of the drug culture. This caused the District's administrators particular concern, since drug use increases the risk of sports-related injury. Expert testimony at the trial confirmed the deleterious effects of drugs on motivation, memory, judgment, reaction, coordination, and performance. The high school football and wrestling coach witnessed a severe sternum injury suffered by a wrestler, and various omissions of safety procedures and misexecutions by football players, all attributable in his belief to the effects of drug use.

Initially, the District responded to the drug problem by offering special classes, speakers, and presentations designed to deter drug use. It even brought in a specially trained dog to detect drugs, but the drug problem persisted. According to the District Court:

> "[T]he administration was at its wits end and . . . a large segment of the student body, particularly those involved in interscholastic athletics, was in a state of rebellion. Disciplinary problems had reached 'epidemic proportions.' The coincidence of an almost three-fold increase in classroom disruptions and disciplinary reports along with the staff's direct observations of students using drugs or glamorizing drug and alcohol use led the administration to the inescapable conclusion that the rebellion was being fueled by alcohol and drug abuse as well as the student's misperceptions about the drug culture."

At that point, District officials began considering a drug-testing program. They held a parent "input night" to discuss the proposed Student Athlete Drug Policy (Policy), and the parents in attendance gave their unanimous approval. The school board approved the policy for implementation in the fall of 1989. Its expressed purpose is to prevent student athletes from using drugs, to protect their health and safety, and to provide drug users with assistance programs.

The Policy applies to all students participating in interscholastic athletics. Students wishing to play sports must sign a form consenting to the testing and must obtain the written consent of their parents. Athletes are tested at the beginning of the season for their sport. In addition, once each week of the season the names of the athletes are placed in a "pool" from which a student, with the supervision of two adults, blindly draws the names of 10% of the athletes for random testing. Those selected are notified and tested that same day, if possible.

The student to be tested completes a specimen control form which bears an assigned number. Prescription medications that the student is taking must be identified by providing a copy of the prescription or a doctor's authorization. The student then enters an empty locker room accompanied by an adult monitor of the same sex. Each boy selected produces a sample at a urinal, remaining fully clothed with his back to the monitor, who stands approximately 12 to 15 feet behind the student. Monitors may (though do not always) watch the student while he produces the sample, and they listen for normal sounds of urination. Girls produce samples in an enclosed bathroom stall, so that they can be heard but not observed. After the sample is produced, it is given to the monitor, who checks it for temperature and tampering and then transfers it to a vial.

The samples are sent to an independent laboratory, which routinely tests them for amphetamines, cocaine, and marijuana. Other drugs, such as LSD, may be screened at the request of the District, but the identity of a particular student does not determine which drugs will be tested. The laboratory's procedures are 99.94% accurate. The District follows strict procedures regarding the chain of custody and access to test results. The laboratory does not know the identity of the students whose samples it tests. It is authorized to mail written test reports only to the superintendent and to provide test results to District personnel by telephone only after the requesting official recites a code confirming his authority. Only the superintendent, principals, and athletic directors have access to test results, and the results are not kept for more than one year.

If a sample tests positive, a second test is administered as soon as possible to confirm the result. If the second test is negative, no further action is taken. If the second test is positive, the athlete's parents are notified, and the school principal convenes a meeting with the student and his parents, at which the student is given the option of (1) participating for six weeks in an assistance program that includes weekly urinalysis, or (2) suffering suspension from athletics for the remainder of the current season and the next athletic season. The student is then retested prior to the start of the next athletic season for which he or she is eligible. The Policy states that a second offense results in automatic imposition of option (2); a third offense in suspension for the remainder of the current season and the next two athletic seasons.

In the fall of 1991, respondent James Acton, then a seventh-grader, signed up to play football at one of the District's grade schools. He was denied participation, however, because he and his parents refused to sign the testing consent forms. The Actons filed suit seeking [an injunction, a court order stopping an action, against] enforcement of the Policy on the grounds that it violated the Fourth and Fourteenth Amendments to the United States Constitution and Article I, Section 9, of the Oregon Constitution. After a bench trial, the District Court . . . dismiss[ed] the action. The United States Court of Appeals for the Ninth Circuit reversed, holding that the Policy violated both the Fourth and Fourteenth Amendments and Article I, Section 9, of the Oregon Constitution. We [agreed to hear the case].

The Fourth Amendment to the United States Constitution provides that the Federal Government shall not violate "[t]he right of the people to be secure in their persons, houses, papers, and effects, against unreasonable searches and seizures. . . ." We have held that the Fourteenth Amendment extends this constitutional guarantee to searches and seizures by state officers, including public school officials. In *Skinner v. Railway Labor Executives' Association*, we held that state-compelled collection and testing of urine, such as that required by the Student Athlete Drug Policy, constitutes a "search" subject to the demands of the Fourth Amendment.

As the text of the Fourth Amendment indicates, the ultimate measure of the constitutionality of a governmental search is "reasonableness." At least in a case such as this, where there was no clear practice, either approving or disapproving the type of search at issue, at the time the constitutional provision was enacted, whether a particular search meets the reasonableness standard "'is judged by balancing its intrusion on the individual's Fourth Amendment interests against its promotion of legitimate governmental interests.'" Where a search is undertaken by law enforcement officials to discover evidence of criminal wrongdoing, this Court has said that reasonableness generally requires the obtaining of a judicial warrant. Warrants cannot be issued, of course, without the showing of probable cause required by the Warrant Clause. But a warrant is not required to establish the reasonableness of *all* government searches; and when a warrant is not required (and the

Warrant Clause therefore not applicable), probable cause is not invariably required either. A search unsupported by probable cause can be constitutional, we have said, "when special needs, beyond the normal need for law enforcement, make the warrant and probable-cause requirement impracticable."

We have found such "special needs" to exist in the public-school context. There, the warrant requirement "would unduly interfere with the maintenance of the swift and informal disciplinary procedures [that are] needed," and "strict adherence to the requirement that searches be based upon probable cause" would undercut "the substantial need of teachers and administrators for freedom to maintain order in the schools." The school search we approved in *T.L.O.*, while not based on probable cause, *was* based on individualized *suspicion* of wrongdoing. As we explicitly acknowledged, however, "'the Fourth Amendment imposes no irreducible requirement of such suspicion.'" We have upheld suspicionless searches and seizures to conduct drug testing of railroad personnel involved in train accidents, to conduct random drug testing of federal customs officers who carry arms or are involved in drug interdiction, and to maintain automobile checkpoints looking for illegal immigrants and contraband, and drunk drivers.

The first factor to be considered is the nature of the privacy interest upon which the search here at issue intrudes. The Fourth Amendment does not protect all subjective expectations of privacy, but only those that society recognizes as "legitimate." What expectations are legitimate varies, of course, with context, depending, for example, upon whether the individual asserting the privacy interest is at home, at work, in a car, or in a public park. In addition, the legitimacy of certain privacy expectations vis-a-vis the State may depend upon the individual's legal relationship with the

State. For example, in *Griffin,* we held that, although a "probationer's home, like anyone else's, is protected by the Fourth Amendmen[t]," the supervisory relationship between probationer and State justifies "a degree of impingement upon [a probationer's] privacy that would not be constitutional if applied to the public at large." Central, in our view, to the present case is the fact that the subjects of the Policy are (1) children, who (2) have been committed to the temporary custody of the State as schoolmaster.

Traditionally at common law, and still today, unemancipated minors lack some of the most fundamental rights of self-determination - including even the right of liberty in its narrow sense, *i.e.,* the right to come and go at will. They are subject, even as to their physical freedom, to the control of their parents as guardians. When parents place minor children in private schools for their education, the teachers and administrators of those schools stand *in loco parentis* [in place of the parents] over the children entrusted to them. In fact, the tutor or schoolmaster is the very prototype of that status. As Blackstone describes it, a parent "may . . . delegate part of his parental authority, during his life, to the tutor or schoolmaster of his child; who is then *in loco parentis,* and has such a portion of the power of the parent committed to his charge, viz., that of restraint and correction, as may be necessary to answer the purposes for which he is employed."

In *T.L.O.* we rejected the notion that public schools, like private schools, exercise only parental power over their students, which of course is not subject to constitutional constraints. Such a view of things, we said, "is not entirely 'consonant with compulsory education laws,'" and is inconsistent with our prior decisions treating school officials as state actors for purposes of the Due Process and Free Speech Clauses. But while denying that the State's power over schoolchildren is formally no more than the delegated power of their parents, *T.L.O.* did not deny, but indeed emphasized, that the nature of that power is custodial and tutelary, permitting a degree of supervision and control that could not be exercised over free adults. "[A] proper educational environment requires close supervision of schoolchildren, as well as the enforcement of rules against conduct that would be perfectly permissible if undertaken by an adult." While we do not, of course, suggest that public schools as a general matter have such a degree of control over children as to give rise to a constitutional "duty to protect," we have acknowledged that for many purposes "school authorities ac[t] *in loco parentis,*" with the power and indeed the duty to "inculcate the habits and manners of civility." Thus, while children assuredly do not "shed their constitutional rights . . . at the schoolhouse gate," the nature of those rights is what is appropriate for children in school.

Fourth Amendment rights, no less than First and Fourteenth Amendment rights, are different in public schools than elsewhere; the "reasonableness" inquiry cannot disregard the schools' custodial and tutelary responsibility for children. For their own good and that of their classmates, public school children are routinely required to submit to various physical examinations, and to be vaccinated against various diseases. According to the American Academy of Pediatrics, most public schools "provide vision and hearing screening and dental and dermatological checks. . . . Others also mandate scoliosis screening at appropriate grade levels." In the 1991-1992 school year, all 50 States required public-school students to be vaccinated against diphtheria, measles, rubella, and polio. Particularly with regard to medical examinations and procedures, therefore, "students within the school environment have a lesser expectation of privacy than members of the population generally."

Legitimate privacy expectations are even less with regard to student athletes. School sports are not for the bashful. They require "suiting up" before each practice or event, and showering and changing afterwards. Public school locker rooms, the usual sites for these activities, are not notable for the privacy they afford. The locker rooms in Vernonia are typical: no individual dressing rooms are provided; shower heads are lined up along a wall, unseparated by any sort of partition or curtain; not even all the toilet stalls have doors. As the United States Court of Appeals for the Seventh Circuit has noted, there is "an element of 'communal undress' inherent in athletic participation."

There is an additional respect in which school athletes have a reduced expectation of privacy. By choosing to "go out for the team," they voluntarily subject themselves to a degree of regulation even higher than that imposed on students generally. In Vernonia's public schools, they must submit to a preseason physical exam (James testified that his included the giving of a urine sample), they must acquire adequate insurance coverage or sign an insurance waiver, maintain a minimum grade point average, and comply with any "rules of conduct, dress, training hours and related matters as may be established for each sport by the head coach and athletic director with the principal's approval." Somewhat like adults who choose to participate in a "closely regulated industry," students who voluntarily participate in school athletics have reason to expect intrusions upon normal rights and privileges, including privacy.

Having considered the scope of the legitimate expectation of privacy at issue here, we turn next to the character of the intrusion that is complained of. We recognized in *Skinner* that collecting the samples for urinalysis intrudes upon "an excretory function traditionally shielded by great privacy." We noted, however, that the degree of intrusion depends upon the manner in which production of the urine sample is monitored. Under the District's Policy, male students produce samples at a urinal along a wall. They remain fully clothed and are only observed from behind, if at all. Female students produce samples in an enclosed stall, with a female monitor standing outside listening only for sounds of tampering. These conditions are nearly identical to those typically encountered in public restrooms, which men, women, and especially school children use daily. Under such conditions, the privacy interests compromised by the process of obtaining the urine sample are in our view negligible.

The other privacy-invasive aspect of urinalysis is, of course, the information it discloses concerning the state of the subject's body, and the materials he has ingested. In this regard it is significant that the tests at issue here look only for drugs, and not for whether the student is, for example, epileptic, pregnant, or diabetic. Moreover, the drugs for which the samples are screened are standard, and do not vary according to the identity of the student. And finally, the results of the tests are disclosed only to a limited class of school personnel who have a need to know; and they are not turned over to law enforcement authorities or used for any internal disciplinary function.

Respondents [the Actons] argue, however, that the District's Policy is in fact more intrusive than this suggests, because it requires the students, if they are to avoid sanctions for a falsely positive test, to identify *in advance* prescription medications they are taking. We agree that this raises some cause for concern. In *Von Raab*, we flagged as one of the salutary features of the Customs Service drug-testing program the fact that employees were not required to disclose medical information unless they tested positive, and, even then, the information was supplied to a licensed physician rather than to the Government employer. On the other hand, we have never indicated that requiring advance disclosure of medications is *per se* unreasonable. Indeed, in *Skinner* we held that it was not "a significant invasion of privacy." It can be argued that, in *Skinner*, the disclosure went only to the medical personnel taking the sample, and the Government personnel analyzing it, and that disclosure to teachers and coaches - to persons who personally *know* the student - is a greater invasion of privacy. Assuming for the sake of argument that both those propositions are true, we do not believe they establish a difference that [the Actons] are entitled to rely on here.

The General Authorization Form that [the Actons] refused to sign, which refusal was the basis for James's exclusion from the sports program, said only (in relevant part): "I . . . authorize the Vernonia School District to conduct a test on a urine specimen which I provide to test for drugs and/or alcohol use. I also authorize the release of information concerning the results of such a test to the Vernonia School District and to the parents and/or guardians of the student." While the practice of the District seems to have been to have a school official take medication information from the student at the time of the test, that practice is not set forth in, or required by, the Policy, which says simply: "Student athletes who . . . are or have been taking prescription medication must provide verification (either by a copy of the prescription or by doctor's authorization) prior to being tested." It may well be that, if and when James was selected for random testing at a time that he was taking medication, the School District would have permitted him to provide the requested information in a confidential manner - for example, in a sealed envelope delivered to the testing lab. Nothing in the Policy contradicts that, and when [the Actons] choose, in effect, to challenge the Policy on its face, we will not assume the worst. Accordingly, we reach the same conclusion as in *Skinner:* that the invasion of privacy was not significant.

Finally, we turn to consider the nature and immediacy of the governmental concern at issue here, and the efficacy of this means for meeting it. In both *Skinner* and *Von Raab*, we characterized the government interest motivating the search as "compelling." Relying on these cases, the District Court held that because the District's program also called for drug testing in the absence of individualized suspicion, the District "must demonstrate a 'compelling need' for the program." The Court of Appeals appears to have agreed with this view. It is a mistake, however, to think that the phrase "compelling state interest," in the Fourth Amendment context, describes a fixed, minimum quantum of governmental concern, so that one can dispose of a case by answering in isolation the question: Is there a compelling state interest here? Rather, the phrase describes an interest which appears *important enough* to justify the particular search at hand, in light of other factors which show the search to be relatively intrusive upon a genuine expectation of privacy. Whether that relatively high degree of government concern is necessary in this case or not, we think it is met.

That the nature of the concern is important - indeed, perhaps compelling - can hardly be doubted. Deterring drug use by our Nation's schoolchildren is at least as important as enhancing efficient enforcement of the Nation's laws against the importation of drugs, which was the governmental concern in *Von Raab*, or deterring drug use by engineers and trainmen, which was the governmental concern in *Skinner.* School years are the time when the physical, psychological, and addictive effects of drugs are most severe. "Maturing nervous systems are more critically impaired by intoxicants than mature ones are; childhood losses in learning are lifelong and profound"; "children grow chemically dependent more quickly than adults, and their record of recovery is depressingly poor." And of course the effects of a drug-infested school are visited not just upon the users, but upon the entire student body and faculty, as the educational process is disrupted. In the present case, moreover, the necessity for the State to act is magnified by the fact that this evil is being visited not just upon individuals at large, but upon children for whom it has undertaken a special responsibility of care and direction. Finally, it must not be lost sight of that this program is directed more narrowly to drug use by school athletes, where the risk of immediate physical harm to the drug user or those with whom he is playing his sport is particularly high. Apart from psychological effects, which include impairment of judgment, slow reaction time, and a lessening of the perception of pain, the particular drugs screened by the District's Policy have been demonstrated to pose substantial physical risks to athletes. Amphetamines produce an "artificially induced heart rate increase, [p]eripheral vasoconstriction, [b]lood pressure increase, and [m]asking of the normal fatigue response," making them a "very dangerous drug when used during exercise of any type." Marijuana causes "[i]rregular blood pressure responses during changes in body position," [r]eduction in the oxygen-carrying capacity of the blood," and "[i]nhibition of the normal sweating responses resulting in increased body temperature." Cocaine produces "[v]asoconstriction[,] [e]levated blood pressure," and "[p]ossible coronary artery spasms and myocardial infarction."

As for the immediacy of the District's concerns: We are not inclined to question - indeed, we could not possibly find clearly erroneous - the District Court's conclusion that "a large segment of the student body, particularly those involved in interscholastic athletics, was in a state of rebellion," that "[d]isciplinary actions had reached 'epidemic proportions,'" and that "the rebellion was being fueled by alcohol and drug abuse as well as by the student's misperceptions about the drug culture." That is an immediate crisis of greater proportions than existed in *Skinner*, where we upheld the Government's drug testing program based on findings of drug use by railroad employees nationwide, without proof that a problem existed on the particular railroads whose employees were subject to the test. And of much greater proportions than existed in *Von Raab*, where there was no documented history of drug use by any customs officials.

As to the efficacy of this means for addressing the problem: It seems to us self-evident that a drug problem largely fueled by the "role model" effect of athletes' drug use, and of particular danger to athletes, is effectively addressed by making sure that athletes do not use drugs. [The Actons] argue that a "less intrusive means to the same end" was available, namely, "drug testing on suspicion of drug use." We have repeatedly refused to declare that only the "least intrusive" search practicable can be reasonable under the Fourth Amendment. [The Actons'] alternative entails substantial difficulties - if it is indeed practicable at all. It may be impracticable, for one thing, simply because the parents who are willing to accept random drug testing for athletes are not willing to accept accusatory drug testing for all students, which transforms the process into a badge of shame. [The Actons'] proposal brings the risk that teachers will impose testing arbitrarily upon troublesome but not drug-likely students. In generates the expense of defending lawsuits that charge such arbitrary imposition, or that simply demand greater process before accusatory drug testing is imposed. And not least of all, it adds to the ever-expanding diversionary duties of schoolteachers the new function of spotting and bringing to account drug abuse, a task for which they are ill prepared, and which is not readily compatible with their vocation. In many respects, we think, testing based on "suspicion" of drug use would not be better, but worse.

Taking into account all the factors we have considered above - the decreased expectation of privacy, the relative unobtrusiveness of the search, and the severity of the need met by the search - we conclude Vernonia's Policy is reasonable and hence constitutional.

We caution against the assumption that suspicionless drug testing will readily pass constitutional muster in other contexts. The most significant element in this case is the first we discussed: that the Policy was undertaken in furtherance of the government's responsibilities, under a public school system, as guardian and tutor of children entrusted to its care. Just as when the government conducts a search in its capacity as employer (a warrantless search of an absent employee's desk to obtain an urgently needed file, for example), the relevant question is whether that intrusion upon privacy is one that a reasonable employer might engage in; so also when the government acts as guardian and tutor the relevant question is whether the search is one that a reasonable guardian and tutor might undertake. Given the findings of need made by the District Court, we conclude that in the present case it is.

We may note that the primary guardians of Vernonia's schoolchildren appear to agree. The record shows no objection to this district-wide program by any parents other than the couple before us here - even though, as we have described, a public meeting was held to obtain parents' views. We find insufficient basis to contradict the judgment of Vernonia's parents, its school board, and the District Court, as to what was reasonably in the interest of these children under the circumstances.

The Ninth Circuit held that Vernonia's Policy not only violated the Fourth Amendment, but also, by reason of that violation, contravened Article I, Section 9 of the Oregon Constitution. Our conclusion that the former holding was in error means that the latter holding rested on a flawed premise. We therefore vacate [annul] the judgment, and remand [return] the case to the Court of Appeals for further proceedings consistent with this opinion.

It is so ordered.

THE U.S. CONSTITUTION

PREAMBLE

We the people of the United States, in order to form a more perfect union, establish justice, insure domestic tranquility, provide for the common defense, promote the general welfare, and secure the blessings of liberty to ourselves and our posterity, do ordain and establish this Constitution for the United States of America.

ARTICLE I

Section 1. All legislative powers herein granted shall be vested in a Congress of the United States, which shall consist of a Senate and House of Representatives.

Section 2. (1) The House of Representatives shall be composed of members chosen every second year by the people of several states, and the electors in each state shall have the qualifications requisite for electors of the most numerous branch of the State Legislature.

(2) No person shall be a Representative who shall not have attained to the age of twenty-five years, and been seven years a citizen of the United States, and who shall not, when elected, be an inhabitant of that state in which he shall be chosen.

(3) Representatives and direct taxes shall be apportioned among the several states which may be included within this union, according to their respective numbers, which shall be determined by adding to the whole number of free persons, including those bound to service for a term of years, and excluding Indians not taxed, three-fifths of all other

persons. The actual enumeration shall be made within three years after the first meeting of the Congress of the United States, and within every subsequent term of ten years, in such manner as they shall by law direct. The number of Representatives shall not exceed one for every thirty thousand, but each state shall have at least one Representative; and until such enumeration shall be made, the State of New Hampshire shall be entitled to choose three, Massachusetts eight, Rhode Island and Providence Plantations one, Connecticut five, New York six, New Jersey four, Pennsylvania eight, Delaware one, Maryland six, Virginia ten, North Carolina five, South Carolina five, and Georgia three.

(4) When vacancies happen in the representation from any state, the executive authority thereof shall issue Writs of Election to fill such vacancies.

(5) The House of Representatives shall choose their Speaker and other Officers; and shall have the sole power of impeachment.

Section 3. (1) The Senate of the United States shall be composed of two Senators from each state, chosen by the legislature thereof, for six years; and each Senator shall have one vote.

(2) Immediately after they shall be assembled in consequence of the first election, they shall be divided as equally as may be into three classes. The seats of the Senators of the first class shall be vacated at the expiration of the second year, of the second class at the expiration of the fourth year, and of the third class at the expiration of the sixth year, so that one-third may be chosen every second year; and if vacancies happen by resignation, or otherwise, during the recess of the legislature of any state, the executive

thereof may make temporary appointments until the next meeting of the legislature, which shall then fill such vacancies.

(3) No person shall be a Senator who shall not have attained to the age of thirty years, and been nine years a citizen of the United States, and who shall not, when elected, be an inhabitant of that state for which he shall be chosen.

(4) The Vice President of the United States shall be President of the Senate, but shall have no vote, unless they be equally divided.

(5) The Senate shall choose their other Officers, and also a President pro tempore, in the absence of the Vice President, or when he shall exercise the Office of President of the United States.

(6) The Senate shall have the sole power to try all impeachments. When sitting for that purpose, they shall be on oath or affirmation. When the President of the United States is tried, the Chief Justice shall preside: and no person shall be convicted without the concurrence of two-thirds of the members present.

(7) Judgment in cases of impeachment shall not extend further than to removal from office, and disqualification to hold and enjoy any office of honor, trust, or profit under the United States: but the party convicted shall nevertheless be liable and subject to indictment, trial, judgment, and punishment, according to law.

Section 4. (1) The times, places and manner of holding elections for Senators and Representatives, shall be prescribed in each state by the legislature thereof; but the Congress may at any time by law make or alter such regulations, except as to the places of choosing Senators.

(2) The Congress shall assemble at least once in every year, and such meeting shall be on the first Monday in December, unless they shall by law appoint a different day.

Section 5. (1) Each House shall be the judge of the elections, returns, and qualifications of its own members, and a majority of each shall constitute a quorum to do business; but a smaller number may adjourn from day to day, and may be authorized to compel the attendance of absent members, in such manner, and under such penalties as each House may provide.

(2) Each House may determine the rules of its proceedings, punish its members for disorderly behavior, and, with the concurrence of two-thirds, expel a member.

(3) Each House shall keep a journal of its proceedings, and from time to time publish the same, excepting such parts as may in their judgment require secrecy; and the yeas and nays of the members of either House on any question shall, at the desire of one-fifth of those present, be entered on the journal.

(4) Neither House, during the Session of Congress, shall, without the consent of the other, adjourn for more than three days, nor to any other place than that in which the two Houses shall be sitting.

Section 6. (1) The Senators and Representatives shall receive a compensation for their services, to be ascertained by law, and paid out of the Treasury of the United States. They shall in all cases, except treason, felony and breach of the peace, be privileged from arrest during their attendance at the session of their respective Houses, and in going to and returning from the same; and for any speech or debate in either House, they shall not be questioned in any other place.

(2) No Senator or Representative shall, during the time for which he was elected, be appointed to any civil office under the authority of the United States, which shall have been created, or the emoluments whereof shall have been increased during such time and no person holding any office under the United States, shall be a member of either House during his continuance in office.

Section 7. (1) All bills for raising revenue shall originate in the House of Representatives; but the Senate may propose or concur with amendments as on other bills.

(2) Every bill which shall have passed the House of Representatives and the Senate, shall, before it become a law, be presented to the President of the United States; if he approve he shall sign it, but if not he shall return it, with his objections to the House in which it shall have originated, who shall enter the objections at large on their journal, and proceed to reconsider it. If after such reconsideration two-thirds of that House shall agree to pass the bill, it shall be sent together with the objections, to the other House, by which it shall likewise be reconsidered, and if approved by two-thirds of that House, it shall become a law. But in all such cases the votes of both Houses shall be determined by yeas and nays, and the names of the persons voting for and against the bill shall be entered on the journal of each House respectively. If any bill shall not be returned by the President within ten days (Sundays excepted) after it shall have been presented to him, the same shall be a law, in like manner as if he had signed it, unless the Congress by their

adjournment prevent its return in which case it shall not be a law.

(3) Every order, resolution, or vote, to which the concurrence of the Senate and House of Representatives may be necessary (except on a question of adjournment) shall be presented to the President of the United States; and before the same shall take effect, shall be approved by him, or being disapproved by him, shall be repassed by two-thirds of the Senate and House of Representatives, according to the rules and limitations prescribed in the case of a bill.

Section 8. (1) The Congress shall have the power to lay and collect taxes, duties, imposts and excises, to pay the debts and provide for the common defense and general welfare of the United States; but all duties, imposts and excises shall be uniform throughout the United States;

(2) To borrow money on the credit of the United States;

(3) To regulate commerce with foreign nations, and among the several states, and with the Indian Tribes;

(4) To establish an uniform Rule of Naturalization, and uniform laws on the subject of bankruptcies throughout the United States;

(5) To coin money, regulate the value thereof, and of foreign coin, and fix the standard of weights and measures;

(6) To provide for the punishment of counterfeiting the securities and current coin of the United States;

(7) To establish Post Offices and Post Roads;

(8) To promote the progress of science and useful arts, by securing for limited times to authors and inventors the exclusive right to their respective writings and discoveries;

(9) To constitute tribunals inferior to the Supreme Court;

(10) To define and punish piracies and felonies committed on the high seas, and offenses against the Law of Nations;

(11) To declare war, grant Letters of Marque and Reprisal, and make rules concerning captures on land and water;

(12) To raise and support armies, but no appropriation of money to that use shall be for a longer term than two years;

(13) To provide and maintain a Navy;

(14) To make rules for the government and regulation of the land and naval forces;

(15) To provide for calling forth the Militia to execute the laws of the Union, suppress insurrections and repel invasions;

(16) To provide for organizing, arming, and disciplining, the Militia, and for governing such part of them as may be employed in the service of the United States, reserving to the states respectively, the appointment of the Officers, and the authority of training the Militia according to the discipline prescribed by Congress;

(17) To exercise exclusive legislation in all cases whatsoever, over such district (not exceeding ten miles square) as may, by cession of particular states, and the acceptance of Congress, become the Seat of the Government of the United States, and to exercise like authority over all places pur-

chased by the consent of the legislature of the state in which the same shall be, for the erection of forts, magazines, arsenals, dockyards, and other needful buildings; and

(18) To make all laws which shall be necessary and proper for carrying into execution the foregoing powers, and all other powers vested by this Constitution in the Government of the United States, or in any Department or Officer thereof.

Section 9. (1) The migration or importation of such persons as any of the states now existing shall think proper to admit, shall not be prohibited by the Congress prior to the year one thousand eight hundred and eight, but a tax or duty may be imposed on such importation, not exceeding ten dollars for each person.

(2) The privilege of the Writ of Habeas Corpus shall not be suspended, unless when in cases of rebellion or invasion the public safety may require it.

(3) No Bill of Attainder or ex post facto law shall be passed.

(4) No capitation, or other direct, tax shall be laid, unless in proportion to the Census or enumeration herein before directed to be taken.

(5) No tax or duty shall be laid on articles exported from any state.

(6) No preference shall be given by any regulation of commerce or revenue to the ports of one state over those of another: nor shall vessels bound to, or from, one state be obliged to enter, clear, or pay duties in another.

(7) No money shall be drawn from the Treasury, but in consequence of appropriations made by law; and a regular statement and account of the receipts and expenditures of all public money shall be published from time to time.

(8) No title of nobility shall be granted by the United States: and no person holding any office of profit or trust under them, shall, without the consent of the Congress, accept of any present, emolument, office, or title, of any kind whatever, from any King, Prince, or foreign State.

Section 10. (1) No state shall enter into any treaty, alliance, or confederation; grant Letter of Marque and Reprisal; coin money; emit bills of credit; make any thing but gold and silver coin a tender in payment of debts; pass any Bill of Attainder, ex post facto law, or law impairing the obligation of contracts, or grant any title of nobility.

(2) No state shall, without the consent of the Congress, lay any imposts or duties on imports or exports, except what may be absolutely necessary for executing its inspection laws: and the net produce of all duties and imposts, laid by any state on imports or exports, shall be for the use of the Treasury of the United States; and all such laws shall be subject to the revision and control of the Congress.

(3) No state shall, without the consent of Congress, lay any duty of tonnage, keep troops, or ships of war in time of peace, enter into any agreement or compact with another state, or with a foreign power, or engage in war, unless actually invaded, or in such imminent danger as will not admit of delay.

ARTICLE II

Section 1. (1) The executive power shall be vested in a President of the United States of America. He shall hold his office during the term of four years, and, together with the Vice President, chosen for the same term, be elected, as follows:

(2) Each state shall appoint, in such manner as the legislature thereof may direct, a number of electors, equal to the whole number of Senators and Representatives to which the state may be entitled in the Congress; but no Senator or Representative, or person holding an office of trust or profit under the United States, shall be appointed an Elector.

(3) The Electors shall meet in their respective states, and vote by ballot for two persons, of whom one at least shall not be an inhabitant of the same state with themselves. And they shall make a list of all the persons voted for, and of the number of votes for each; which list they shall sign and certify, and transmit sealed to the Seat of the Government of the United States, directed to the President of the Senate. The President of the Senate shall, in the presence of the Senate and House of Representatives, open all the certificates, and the votes shall then be counted. The person having the greatest number of votes shall be the President, if such number be a majority of the whole number of Electors appointed; and if there be more than one who have such majority, and have an equal number of votes, then the House of Representatives shall immediately choose by ballot one of them for President; and if no person have a majority, then from the five highest on the list the said House shall in like manner choose the President. But in choosing the President, the votes shall be taken by states the representation from each state having one vote; a

quorum for this purpose shall consist of a member or members from two-thirds of the states, and a majority of all the states shall be necessary to a choice. In every case, after the choice of the President, the person having the greater number of votes of the Electors shall be the Vice President. But if there should remain two or more who have equal votes, the Senate shall choose from them by ballot the Vice President.

(4) The Congress may determine the time of choosing the Electors, and the day on which they shall give their votes; which day shall be the same throughout the United States.

(5) No person except a natural born citizen, or a citizen of the United States, at the time of the adoption of this Constitution, shall be eligible to the Office of President; neither shall any person be eligible to that Office who shall not have attained to the age of thirty-five years, and been fourteen years a resident within the United States.

(6) In case of the removal of the President from Office, or of his death, resignation or inability to discharge the powers and duties of the said Office, the same shall devolve on the Vice President, and the Congress may by law provide for the case of removal, death, resignation, or inability, both of the President and Vice President, declaring what Officer shall then act as President, and such Officer shall act accordingly, until the disability be removed, or a President shall be elected.

(7) The President shall, at stated times, receive for his services, a compensation, which shall neither be increased nor diminished during the period for which he shall have been elected, and he shall not receive within that period any other emolument from the United States, or any of them.

(8) Before he enter on the execution of his Office, he shall take the following Oath or Affirmation: "I do solemnly swear (or affirm) that I will faithfully execute the Office of President of the United States, and will to the best of my ability, preserve, protect and defend the Constitution of the United States."

Section 2. (1) The President shall be Commander in Chief of the Army and Navy of the United States, and of the militia of the several states, when called into the actual service of the United States; he may require the opinion, in writing, of the principal Officer in each of the Executive Departments, upon any subject relating to the duties of their respective Offices, and he shall have power to grant reprieves and pardons for offenses against the United States, except in cases of impeachment.

(2) He shall have power, by and with the advice and consent of the Senate to make treaties, provided two-thirds of the Senators present concur; and he shall nominate, and by and with the advice and consent of the Senate, shall appoint Ambassadors, other public Ministers and Consuls, Judges of the supreme Court, and all other Officers of the United States, whose appointments are not herein otherwise provided for, and which shall be established by law; but the Congress may by law vest the appointment of such inferior Officers, as they think proper, in the President alone, in the courts of law, or in the Heads of Departments.

(3) The President shall have power to fill up all vacancies that may happen during the recess of the Senate, by granting commissions which shall expire at the end of their next Session.

Section 3. He shall from time to time give to the Congress information of the State of the Union, and recommend to their consideration such measures as he shall judge necessary and expedient; he may, on extraordinary occasions, convene both Houses, or either of them, and in case of disagreement between them, with respect to the time of adjournment, he may adjourn them to such time as he shall think proper; he shall receive Ambassadors and other public Ministers; he shall take care that the laws be faithfully executed, and shall commission all the Officers of the United States.

Section 4. The President, Vice President and all civil Officers of the United States, shall be removed from office on impeachment for, and conviction of, treason, bribery, or other high crimes and misdemeanors.

ARTICLE III

Section 1. The judicial power of the United States, shall be vested in one supreme Court, and in such inferior courts as the Congress may from time to time ordain and establish. The Judges, both of the supreme and inferior courts, shall hold their Offices during good behaviour, and shall, at stated times, receive for their services a compensation, which shall not be diminished during their continuance in office.

Section 2. (1) The judicial power shall extend to all cases, in law and equity, arising under this Constitution, the laws of the United States, and treaties made, or which shall be made, under their authority; to all cases affecting Ambassadors, other public Ministers and Consuls; to all cases of admiralty and maritime jurisdiction; to controversies to which the United States shall be a party; to controversies between two or more states; between a state and citizens of another state; between citizens of different states; between citizens of the same state claiming lands under the grants of different states, and between a state, or the citizens thereof, and foreign states, citizens or subjects.

(2) In all cases affecting Ambassadors, other public Ministers and Consuls, and those in which a state shall be a party, the supreme Court shall have original jurisdiction. In all the other cases before mentioned, the supreme Court shall have appellate jurisdiction, both as to law and fact, with such exceptions, and under such regulations as the Congress shall make.

(3) The trial of all crimes, except in cases of impeachment, shall be by jury; and such trial shall be held in the state where the said crimes shall have been committed; but when not committed within any state, the trial shall be at such place or places as the Congress may by law have directed.

Section 3. (1) Treason against the United States, shall consist only in levying war against them, or, in adhering to their enemies, giving them aid and comfort. No person shall be convicted of treason unless on the testimony of two witnesses to the same overt act, or on confession in open Court.

(2) The Congress shall have power to declare the punishment of treason, but no Attainder of Treason shall work corruption of blood, or forfeiture except during the life of the person attainted.

ARTICLE IV

Section 1. Full faith and credit shall be given in each state to the public acts, records, and judicial proceedings of every other state. And the Congress may by general laws prescribe the manner in which such acts, records and proceedings shall be proved, and the effect thereof.

Section 2. (1) The citizens of each state shall be entitled to all privileges and immunities of citizens in the several states.

(2) A person charged in any state with treason, felony, or other crime, who shall flee from justice, and be found in another state, shall on demand of the executive authority of the state from which he fled, be delivered up, to be removed to the state having jurisdiction of the crime.

(3) No person held to service or labour in one state, under the laws thereof, escaping into another, shall, in consequence of any law or regulation therein, be discharged from such service or labour, but shall be delivered up on claim of the party to whom such service or labour may be due.

Section 3. (1) New states may be admitted by the Congress into this Union; but no new state shall be formed or erected within the jurisdiction of any other state; nor any state be formed by the junction of two or more states, or parts of states, without the consent of the legislatures of the states concerned as well as of the Congress.

(2) The Congress shall have power to dispose of and make all needful rules and regulations respecting the territory or other property belonging to the United States; and nothing in this Constitution shall be so construed as to prejudice any claims of the United States, or of any particular state.

Section 4. The United States shall guarantee to every state in this Union a Republican form of government, and shall protect each of them against invasion; and on application of the Legislature, or of the Executive (when the Legislature cannot be convened) against domestic violence.

ARTICLE V

The Congress, whenever two-thirds of both Houses shall deem it necessary, shall propose amendments to this Constitution, or, on the application of the Legislatures of two-thirds of the several states, shall call a convention for proposing amendments, which, in either case, shall be valid to all intents and purposes, as part of this constitution, when ratified by the Legislatures of three-fourths of the several states, or by conventions in three-fourths thereof, as the one or the other mode of ratification may be proposed by the Congress; provided that no amendment which may be made prior to the year one thousand eight hundred and eight shall in any manner affect the first and fourth clauses in the Ninth Section of the first Article; and that no state, without its consent, shall be deprived of its equal suffrage in the Senate.

ARTICLE VI

(1) All debts contracted and engagements entered into, before the adoption of this Constitution shall be as valid against the United States under this Constitution, as under the Confederation.

(2) This Constitution, and the laws of the United States which shall be made in pursuance thereof; and all treaties made, or which shall be made, under the authority of the United States, shall be the supreme law of the land; and the Judges in every state shall be bound thereby, any thing in the Constitution or laws of any state to the contrary notwithstanding.

(3) The Senators and Representatives before mentioned, and the Members of the several State Legislatures, and all executive and judicial Officers, both of the United States

and of the several states, shall be bound by oath or affirmation, to support this Constitution; but no religious test shall ever be required as a qualification to any Office or public trust under the United States.

ARTICLE VII

The ratification of the Conventions of nine states shall be sufficient for the establishment of this Constitution between the states so ratifying the same.

AMENDMENT I (1791)

Congress shall make no law respecting an establishment of religion, or prohibiting the free exercise thereof; or abridging the freedom of speech, or of the press; or the right of the people peaceably to assemble, and to petition the Government for a redress of grievances.

AMENDMENT II (1791)

A well regulated Militia, being necessary to the security of a free State, the right of the people to keep and bear arms, shall not be infringed.

AMENDMENT III (1791)

No soldier shall, in time of peace be quartered in any house, without the consent of the owner, nor in time of war, but in a manner to be prescribed by law.

AMENDMENT IV (1791)

The right of the people to be secure in their persons, houses, papers, and effects, against unreasonable searches and seizures, shall not be violated, and no warrants shall issue, but upon probable cause, supported by oath or affirmation, and particularly describing the place to be searched, and the persons or things to be seized.

AMENDMENT V (1791)

No person shall be held to answer for a capital, or otherwise infamous crime, unless on a presentment or indictment of a Grand Jury, except in cases arising in the land or naval forces, or in the Militia, when in actual service in time of war or public danger; nor shall any person be subject for the same offense to be twice put in jeopardy of life or limb; nor shall be compelled in any criminal case to be a witness against himself, nor be deprived of life, liberty, or property, without due process of law; nor shall private property be taken for public use, without just compensation.

AMENDMENT VI (1791)

In all criminal prosecutions, the accused shall enjoy the right to a speedy and public trial, by an impartial jury of the state and district wherein the crime shall have been committed, which district shall have been previously ascertained by law, and to be informed of the nature and cause of the accusation; to be confronted with the witnesses against him; to have compulsory process for obtaining witnesses in his favor, and to have the assistance of counsel for his defense.

AMENDMENT VII (1791)

In suits at common law, where the value in controversy shall exceed twenty dollars, the right of trial by jury shall be preserved, and no fact tried by jury, shall be otherwise reexamined in any Court of the United States, than according to the rules of the common law.

AMENDMENT VIII (1791)

Excessive bail shall not be required, nor excessive fines imposed, nor cruel and unusual punishments inflicted.

AMENDMENT IX (1791)

The enumeration in the Constitution, of certain rights, shall not be construed to deny or disparage others retained by the people.

AMENDMENT X (1791)

The powers not delegated to the United States by the Constitution, nor prohibited by it to the States, are reserved to the States respectively, or to the people.

AMENDMENT XI (1798)

The judicial power of the United States shall not be construed to extend to any suit in law or equity, commenced or prosecuted against one of the United States by citizens of another state, or by citizens or subjects of any foreign state.

AMENDMENT XII (1804)

The Electors shall meet in their respective states and vote by ballot for President and Vice-President, one of whom, at least, shall not be an inhabitant of the same state with themselves; they shall name in their ballots the person voted for as President, and in distinct ballots the person voted for as Vice-President, and they shall make distinct lists of all persons voted for as President, and of all persons voted for as Vice-President, and of the number of votes for each, which lists they shall sign and certify, and transmit sealed to the seat of the government of the United States, directed to the President of the Senate; the President of the

Senate shall, in the presence of the Senate and House of Representatives, open all the certificates and the votes shall then be counted; the person having the greatest number of votes for President, shall be the President, if such number be a majority of the persons having the highest numbers not exceeding three on the list of those voted for as President, the House of Representatives shall choose immediately, by ballot, the President. But in choosing the President, the votes shall be taken by states, the representation from each state having one vote; a quorum for this purpose shall consist of a member or members from two-thirds of the states, and a majority of all the states shall be necessary to a choice. And if the House of Representatives shall not choose a President whenever the right of choice shall devolve upon them before the fourth day of March next following, then the Vice-President shall act as President, as in the case of the death or other constitutional disability of the President. The person having the greatest number of votes as Vice-President, shall be the Vice-President, if such number be a majority of the whole number of Electors appointed, and if no person have a majority, then from the two highest numbers on the list, the Senate shall choose the Vice-President; a quorum for the purpose shall consist of two-thirds of the whole number of Senators, and a majority of the whole number shall be necessary to a choice. But no person constitutionally ineligible to the office of President shall be eligible to that of Vice-President of the United States.

AMENDMENT XIII (1865)

Section 1. Neither slavery nor involuntary servitude, except as a punishment for crime whereof the party shall have been duly convicted, shall exist within the United States, or any place subject to their jurisdiction.

Section 2. Congress shall have power to enforce this article by appropriate legislation.

AMENDMENT XIV (1868)

Section 1. All persons born or naturalized in the United States, and subject to the jurisdiction thereof, are citizens of the United States and of the state wherein they reside. No state shall make or enforce any law which shall abridge the privileges or immunities of citizens of the United States; nor shall any state deprive any person of life, liberty, or property, without due process of law; nor deny to any person within its jurisdiction the equal protection of the laws.

Section 2. Representatives shall be apportioned among the several states according to their respective numbers, counting the whole number of persons in each State excluding Indians not taxed. But when the right to vote at any election for the choice of electors for President and Vice President of the United States, Representatives in Congress, the Executive and Judicial officers of a state, or the members of the Legislature thereof, is denied to any of the male inhabitants of such state, being twenty-one years of age, and citizens of the United States, or in any way abridged, except for participation in rebellion, or other crime, the basis of representation therein shall be reduced in the proportion which the number of such male citizens shall bear to the whole number of male citizens twenty-one years of age in such state.

Section 3. No person shall be a Senator or Representative in Congress, or elector of President and Vice President, or hold any office, civil or military, under the United States, or under any state, who having previously taken an oath, as a member of Congress, or as an officer of the United States, or as a member of any state legislature, or as an executive or judicial officer of any state, to support the Constitution of the United States, shall have engaged in insurrection or rebellion against the same, or given aid or comfort to the enemies thereof. But Congress may by a vote of two-thirds of each House, remove such disability.

Section 4. The validity of the public debt of the United States, authorized by law, including debts incurred for payment of pensions and bounties for services in suppressing insurrection or rebellion, shall not be questioned. But neither the United States nor any state shall assume or pay any debt or obligation incurred in aid of insurrection or rebellion against the United States, or any claim for the loss or emancipation of any slave; but all such debts, obligations and claims shall be held illegal and void.

Section 5. The Congress shall have power to enforce, by appropriate legislation, the provisions of this article.

AMENDMENT XV (1870)

Section 1. The right of citizens of the United States to vote shall not be denied or abridged by the United States or by any state on account of race, color, or previous condition of servitude.

Section 2. The Congress shall have power to enforce this article by appropriate legislation.

AMENDMENT XVI (1913)

The Congress shall have power to lay and collect taxes on income, from whatever source derived, without apportionment among the several states, and without regard to any census or enumeration.

AMENDMENT XVII (1913)

(1) The Senate of the United States shall be composed of two Senators from each state, elected by the people thereof, for six years; and each Senator shall have one vote. The electors in each State shall have the qualifications requisite for electors of the most numerous branch of the state legislatures.

(2) When vacancies happen in the representation of any state in the Senate, the executive authority of such state shall issue writs of election to fill such vacancies: provided, that the legislature of any state may empower the executive thereof to make temporary appointments until the people fill the vacancies by election as the legislature may direct.

(3) This amendment shall not be so construed as to affect the election or term of any Senator chosen before it becomes valid as part of the Constitution.

AMENDMENT XVIII (1919)

Section 1. After one year from the ratification of this article the manufacture, sale, or transportation of intoxicating liquors within, the importation thereof into, or the exportation thereof from the United States and all territory subject to the jurisdiction thereof for beverage purposes is hereby prohibited.

Section 2. The Congress and the several states shall have concurrent power to enforce this article by appropriate legislation.

Section 3. This article shall be inoperative unless it shall have been ratified as an amendment to the Constitution by the legislatures of the several states, as provided in the Constitution, within seven years from the date of the submission hereof to the states by the Congress.

AMENDMENT XIX (1920)

(1) The right of citizens of the United States to vote shall not be denied or abridged by the United States or by any state on account of sex.

(2) Congress shall have power to enforce this article by appropriate legislation.

AMENDMENT XX (1933)

Section 1. The terms of the President and Vice President shall end at noon on the 20th day of January, and the terms of Senators and Representatives at noon on the 3d day of January, of the years in which such terms would have ended if this article had not been ratified; and the terms of their successors shall then begin.

Section 2. The Congress shall assemble at least once in every year, and such meeting shall begin at noon on the 3d day of January, unless they shall by law appoint a different day.

Section 3. If, at the time fixed for the beginning of the term of the President, the President elect shall have died, the Vice President elect shall become President. If the President shall not have been chosen before the time fixed for the beginning of his term, or if the President elect shall have failed to qualify, then the Vice President elect shall act as President until a President shall have qualified; and the Congress may by law provide for the case wherein neither a President elect nor a Vice President elect shall have qualified, declaring who shall then act as President, or the manner in which one who is to act shall be selected, and such person shall act accordingly until a President or Vice President shall have qualified.

Section 4. The Congress may by law provide for the case of the death of any of the persons from whom the House of Representatives may choose a President whenever the right of choice shall have devolved upon them, and for the case of the death of any of the persons from whom the Senate may choose a Vice President whenever the right of choice shall have devolved upon them.

Section 5. Sections 1 and 2 shall take effect on the 15th day of October following the ratification of this article.

Section 6. This article shall be inoperative unless it shall have been ratified as an amendment to the Constitution by the legislatures of three-fourths of the several states within seven years from the date of its submission.

AMENDMENT XXI (1933)

Section 1. The eighteenth article of amendment to the Constitution of the United States is hereby repealed.

Section 2. The transportation or importation into any state, territory, or possession of the United States for delivery or use therein of intoxicating liquors, in violation of the laws thereof, is hereby prohibited.

Section 3. This article shall be inoperative unless it shall have been ratified as an amendment to the Constitution by conventions in the several states, as provided in the Constitution, within seven years from the date of the submission hereof to the states by the Congress.

AMENDMENT XXII (1951)

Section 1. No person shall be elected to the office of the President more than twice, and no person who has held the office of President, or acted as President, for more than two years of a term to which some other person was elected President shall be elected to the office of President more than once. But this Article shall not apply to any person holding the office of President when this Article was proposed by the Congress, and shall not prevent any person who may be holding the office of President, or acting as President, during the term within which this Article becomes operative from holding the office of President or acting as President during the remainder of such term.

Section 2. This article shall be inoperative unless it shall have been ratified as an amendment to the Constitution by the legislatures of three-fourths of the several states within seven years from the date of its submission to the states by the Congress.

AMENDMENT XXIII (1961)

Section 1. The District constituting the seat of Government of the United States shall appoint in such manner as the Congress may direct:

A number of electors of President and Vice President equal to the whole number of Senators and Representatives in Congress to which the District would be entitled if it were a state, but in no event more than the least populous state; they shall be in addition to those appointed by the states, but they shall be considered, for the purposes of the election of President and Vice President, to be electors appointed by a state; and they shall meet in the District and perform such duties as provided by the twelfth article of amendment.

Section 2. The Congress shall have power to enforce this article by appropriate legislation.

AMENDMENT XXIV (1964)

Section 1. The right of citizens of the United States to vote in any primary or other election for President or Vice President, for electors for President or Vice President, or for Senator or Representative in Congress, shall not be denied or abridged by the United States, or any state by reason of failure to pay any poll tax or other tax.

Section 2. The Congress shall have power to enforce this article by appropriate legislation.

AMENDMENT XXV (1967)

Section 1. In case of the removal of the President from office or of his death or resignation, the Vice President shall become President.

Section 2. Whenever there is a vacancy in the office of the Vice President, the President shall nominate a Vice President who shall take office upon confirmation by a majority vote of both Houses of Congress.

Section 3. Whenever the President transmits to the President pro tempore of the Senate and the Speaker of the House of Representatives his written declaration that he is unable to discharge the powers and duties of his office, and until he transmits to them a written declaration to the contrary, such powers and duties shall be discharged by the Vice President as Acting President.

Section 4. Whenever the Vice President and a majority of either the principal officers of the executive departments or of such other body as Congress may by law provide, transmit to the President pro tempore of the Senate and the Speaker of the House of Representatives their written declaration that the President is unable to discharge the powers and duties of his office, the Vice President shall immediately assume the powers and duties of the office as Acting President.

Thereafter, when the President transmits to the President pro tempore of the Senate and the Speaker of the House of Representatives his written declaration that no inability exists, he shall resume the powers and duties of his office unless the Vice President and a majority of either the principal officers of the executive department or of such other body as Congress may by law provide, transmit within four days to the President pro tempore of the Senate and the Speaker of the House of Representatives their written declaration that the President is unable to discharge the powers and duties of his office. Thereupon Congress shall decide the issue, assembling within forty-eight hours for that purpose if not in session. If the Congress, within twenty-one days after receipt of the latter written declaration, or, if Congress is not in session, within twenty-one days after Congress is required to assemble, determines by two-thirds vote of both Houses that the President is unable to discharge the power and duties of his office, the Vice President shall continue to discharge the same as Acting President; otherwise, the President shall resume the powers and duties of his office.

AMENDMENT XXVI (1971)

Section 1. The right of citizens of the United States, who are eighteen years of age or older, to vote shall not be denied or abridged by the United States or by any state on account of age.

Section 2. The Congress shall have power to enforce this article by appropriate legislation.

AMENDMENT XXVII (1992)

No law, varying the compensation for the services of the Senators and Representatives, shall take effect, until an election of Representatives shall have intervened.

BIBLIOGRAPHY

Agresto, John. *The Supreme Court and Constitutional Democracy.* Ithaca, NY: Cornell University Press, 1984.

Alley, Robert S. *School Prayer: the Court, the Congress, and the First Amendment.* Buffalo, NY: Prometheus Books, 1984.

Anonymous. *Go Ask Alice.* New York, NY: Avon Books, 1982.

Berra, Tim M. *Evolution and the Myth of Creationism.* Stanford, CA: Stanford University Press, 1990.

Blaustein, Albert P. and Clarence C. Ferguson, Jr. *Desegregation and the Law: The Meaning of the School Segregation Cases.* New Brunswick, NJ: Rutgers University Press, 1957.

Bosmajian, Haig A. *The Freedom to Read.* New York, NY: Neal-Schuman, 1987.

Burress, Lee. *Battle of the Books: Literary Censorship in the Public Schools, 1950-1985.* Metuchen, NJ: Scarecrow Press, 1989.

Childress, Alice. *A Hero Ain't Nothin' But A Sandwich.* New York, NY: Coward McCann, 1973.

Cleaver, Eldridge. *Soul on Ice.* New York, NY: McGraw-Hill, 1968.

Cox, Archibald. *The Court and the Constitution.* New York, NY: Houghton-Mifflin, 1988.

Darwin, Charles. *The Origin of Species.* New York, NY: Literary Classics, 1900.

DelFattore, Joan. *What Johnny Shouldn't Read: Textbook Censorship in America*. New Haven, CT: Yale University Press, 1992.

Dolbeare, Kenneth M., and Phillip E. Hammond. *The School Prayer Decisions From Court Policy to Local Practice*. Chicago, IL: University of Chicago Press, 1971.

Dumbauld, Edward. *The Bill of Rights and What It Means Today*. New York, NY: Greenwood Press, 1979.

Fenwick, Lynda B. *Should the Children Pray? A Historical, Judicial, and Political Examination of Public School Prayer*. Waco, TX: Baylor University Press, 1989.

Ginger, Ann Fagan. *The Law, The Supreme Court, and The People's Rights*. Woodbury, NY: Barron's Educational Series, 1973.

Goode, Stephen. *The Controversial Court: Supreme Court Influences on American Life*. New York, NY: Messner, 1982.

Hughes, Langston, Editor. *The Best Short Stories of Negro Writers*. Boston, MA: Little, Brown, 1967.

Kik, Jacob M. *The Supreme Court and Prayer in the Public School*. Philadelphia, PA: Presbyterian and Reformed Publishing Company, 1963.

LaFarge, Oliver. *Laughing Boy*. New York, NY: Houghton-Mifflin, 1929.

Larson, Edward J. *Trial and Error: The American Controversy Over Creation and Evolution*. New York, NY: Oxford University Press, 1985.

Lawson, Don. *Landmark Supreme Court Cases*. Hillside, NJ: Enslow Publishers, Inc., 1987.

Manwering, David R. *Render Unto Caesar: The Flag-Salute Controversy*. Chicago, IL: University of Chicago Press, 1962.

Morris, Desmond. *The Naked Ape*. New York, NY: McGraw-Hill, 1967.

Murray, William J. *Let Us Pray: A Plea for Prayer in our Schools*. New York, NY: W. Morrow, 1995.

Noble, William. *Bookbanning in America: Who Bans Books? And Why?* Middlebury, VT: P.S. Eriksson, 1990.

O'Hair, Madalyn Murray. *An Atheist Epic: The Complete Unexpurgated Story of How the Bible and Prayers Were Removed From the Public Schools of the United States*. Austin, TX: American Atheist Press, 1989.

Rehnquist, William H. *The Supreme Court: How It Was, How It Is*. New York, NY: Morrow, 1987.

Stevens, Leonard A. *Salute! The Case of the Bible vs. The Flag*. New York, NY: Coward, McCann & Geoghegan, 1973.

Swanson, June. *I Pledge Allegiance*. Minneapolis, MN: Carolrhoda Books, 1990.

Thomas, Piri. *Down These Mean Streets*. New York, NY: Knopf, 1967.

Vonnegut, Kurt. *Slaughterhouse Five*. New York, NY: Delacorte Press, 1994.

Wilkinson, J. Harvie III, *From Brown to Bakke: The Supreme Court and School Integration, 1954-1978*. New York, NY: Oxford University Press, 1979.

Wolters, Raymond. *The Burden of Brown: Thirty Years of School Desegregation*. Knoxville, TN: The University of Tennessee Press, 1984.

Woodward, Bob, and Scott Armstrong. *The Brethren: Inside the Supreme Court*. New York, NY: Simon & Schuster, 1979.

Wright, Richard. *Black Boy*. New York, NY: Caedmon, 1989.

Zetterberg, J. Peter. *Evolution vs. Creationism*. Phoenix, AZ: The Oryx Press, 1983.

Index

EXCELLENT BOOKS ORDER FORM

(Please xerox this form so it will be available to other readers.)

Please send
Copy(ies)

_____ of SCHOOLHOUSE DECISIONS @ $16.95
_____ of LIFE, DEATH, AND THE LAW @ $16.95
_____ of FREEDOM OF SPEECH DECISIONS @ $16.95
_____ of FREEDOM OF THE PRESS DECISIONS @ $16.95
_____ of FREEDOM OF RELIGION DECISIONS @ $16.95
_____ of THE MURDER REFERENCE @ $16.95
_____ of THE RAPE REFERENCE @ $16.95
_____ of LANDMARK DECISIONS @ $16.95
_____ of LANDMARK DECISIONS II @ $16.95
_____ of LANDMARK DECISIONS III @ $16.95
_____ of LANDMARK DECISIONS IV @ $16.95
_____ of LANDMARK DECISIONS V @ $16.95
_____ of ABORTION DECISIONS: THE 1970's @ $16.95
_____ of ABORTION DECISIONS: THE 1980's @ $16.95
_____ of ABORTION DECISIONS: THE 1990's @ $16.95
_____ of CIVIL RIGHTS DECISIONS: 19th CENTURY @ $16.95
_____ of CIVIL RIGHTS DECISIONS: 20th CENTURY @ $16.95
_____ of THE ADA HANDBOOK @ $16.95

Name: _____

Address: _____

City: _____ State: _____ Zip: _____

Add $1 per book for shipping and handling.
California residents add sales tax.

OUR GUARANTEE: Any Excellent Book may be returned at
any time for any reason and a full refund will be made.

Mail your check or money order to: Excellent Books,
Post Office Box 927105, San Diego, California 92192-7105
or call/fax (760) 598-5069